Music Express

Year 5

LESSON PLANS, RECORDINGS, ACTIVITIES, PHOTOCOPIABLES AND VIDEOCLIPS

Compiled by **Maureen Hanke** with **Xanthe Jarjou, Ana Sanderson, Barry Gibson** and **Sheena Roberts**

Illustrated by **Alison Dexter**   Edited by **Emily Haward** and **Sheena Roberts**

A & C Black • London

D0514432

Contents

Page

First published 2003
Reprinted 2003 (twice), 2006, 2008
by A&C Black Publishers Ltd
36 Soho Square, London W1D 3QY
© 2003 A&C Black Publishers Ltd
ISBN: 978-0-7136-6228-3

Teaching text © 2003 Maureen Hanke, Xanthe Jarjou,
Ana Sanderson and Barry Gibson
Unit headings, unit summary text, learning objectives and
outcomes © Qualifications and Curriculum Authority, 2000
CD/Videoclips compilation © 2003 A&C Black
Edited by Emily Haward and Sheena Roberts
Designed by Jocelyn Lucas
Cover illustration © 2002 Alex Ayliffe
Inside illustrations © 2003 Alison Dexter
Music setting by Jenny Fisher
Audio CD sound engineering by Stephen Chadwick
Videoclips filmed and edited by Jamie Acton-Bond
CD-ROM post production by Ian Shepherd at Sound Recording
Technology

Printed in Great Britain by Caligraving Ltd, Thetford, Norfolk

This book is produced using paper that is made from wood grown
in managed, sustainable forests. It is natural, renewable and recy-
clable. The logging and manufacturing processes conform to the
environmental regulations of the country of origin.

A CIP catalogue record for this book is available from the British
Library.

Introduction

About Music Express

Music Express provides teaching activities that are imaginative, inspiring and fun.

It has been written especially for classroom teachers. It is:

- user-friendly;
- well planned;
- fully resourced, and
- no music reading is required.

Using Music Express as a scheme of work

National Curriculum

Music Express fulfils the requirements of the Music National Curriculum of England, of Wales and of Northern Ireland and the 5-14 National Guidelines for Scotland.

Learning with *Music Express*, children will gain a broad and balanced musical education. They will:

- learn about and sing songs from around the world including the British Isles;
- learn about music from different periods and genres;
- enjoy music lessons with a balance of listening, composing, performing and appraising.

A steady progression plan has been built into *Music Express*, both within each book and from one year to the next, ensuring consistent musical development.

Opportunities are identified throughout for evaluating the children's work and monitoring their progress.

The English QCA scheme of work for music

Music Express is based on the structure of the QCA scheme of work. It uses the same unit headings, and provides activities for all the learning objectives and outcomes.

The teaching activities in *Music Express* have been drawn from and inspired by A & C Black's extensive classroom music resources.

The units

There are six units in each book. Below is a list of the units in *Music Express Year 5*, as described by the QCA:

Cyclic patterns
'This unit develops pupils' ability to perform rhythmic patterns confidently and with a strong sense of pulse.'

Roundabout
'This unit develops children's ability to sing and play music in two (or more) parts. They explore the effect of two or more pitched notes sounding together – harmony. They experiment with clusters of pitched notes and discover which combinations are 'comfortable' (concords), and which 'clash' (discords). They sing rounds and experiment with melodic ostinati to provide accompaniments. They play drones and single note accompaniments.'

Journey into space
'This unit develops children's ability to extend their sound vocabulary, including the use of ICT, and to compose a soundscape.'

Songwriter
'This unit develops children's ability to compose a song with an awareness of the relationship between lyrics and melody.'

Stars, hide your fires
'This unit develops and demonstrates children's ability to take part in a class performance with confidence, expression and control.'

Who knows?
'This unit provides an opportunity for children to develop and demonstrate the musical skills, knowledge and understanding achieved in years 5 and 6.'

There are three activities per lesson which may be taught in one longer music lesson, or over three shorter lessons to suit your timetable.

Planning

The CD-ROM

The CD-ROM provides a medium term plan and six, weekly lesson plans for each unit. These may be printed out to go in your planning folder.

Whilst it is not necessary when teaching the activities to have the lesson plan alongside, it contains useful information for preparing your lesson. This includes:

- the learning objectives and outcomes;

- a list of the resources and minimal preparation you will need to do before the lesson;

- a list of the musical vocabulary appropriate to the lesson (see glossary for definitions);

- a suggestion of ways to provide differentiated support for particular activities;

- a lesson extension – a suggestion for taking the lesson further with individuals or the whole class. (The extension activities are particularly useful when teaching a mixed year-group class as they extend the older and/or more able children.)

The book

The book provides step by step teaching notes for each lesson. These are written to be as easy to follow as possible.

There are photocopiables to supplement many of the activities.

Preparation

Music Express is designed to minimise your preparation time.

Look out for the icons next to the activity headings which indicate things you need to prepare.

Key to icons

 Photocopiable icon: some activities require photocopies or activity cards to be made from a particular photocopiable.

 CD icon: you will need to have access to a CD player for an activity.

 Videoclip and picture icons: you will need to have access to a computer for an activity to show videoclips and pictures on the CD-ROM. (You might like to use a computer-compatible projector to show the videoclips and pictures on a screen for the whole class to see more easily.)

 Notebook icon: unit 4 requires pages from the CD-ROM to make up a songwriter's notebook.

 Music icon: sheet music for the associated song is found on the CD-ROM.

Other resources

Classroom percussion

You will need to have a range of classroom percussion instruments available.

Many activities suggest several members of the class playing instruments at the same time. If necessary, pupils could share instruments and take turns to play.

Specific activities recommend the instruments you will need, but you should use the instruments that you have available.

For a class of 30 pupils, aim to have at least the following:

- Tuned percussion

    1 alto xylophone

    1 alto metallophone

    1 set of chime bars

    a selection of beaters

- A range of untuned percussion instruments, eg

    tambours

    drums

    wood blocks

    cabassas

    maracas

    electronic keyboards (at least one)

- Other interesting soundmakers, eg

    ocean drum

    rainmaker

    whistles

    wind chimes

- Electronic keyboards are a very useful resource and should be included whenever possible.

Instrumental lessons

Whenever appropriate, invite members of the class who are having instrumental lessons to bring their instruments into classroom music lessons.

If you are not sure which notes particular instruments use, ask the child's instrumental teacher.

Recording and evaluating

Recording on cassette or video

Have a cassette recorder and blank audio cassettes available during your music lessons. Recording pupils' work is important for monitoring their progress.

Children enjoy listening to their performances and contributing to the evaluation of their own and their classmates' work.

Many activities include movement as well as music. If you have a video camera available, video the performance. If not, invite members of your class or another class to watch and offer feedback.

Help for teachers

Teaching tips and background information

These are provided throughout next to the activity or activities to which they refer.

Dance and movement

Encourage movement in activities where it is not mentioned – it is an important means of musical learning.

Group work

The activities suggest appropriate group sizes. Be flexible, especially if your class has little or no experience of group work. Group work may be introduced into classroom music lessons gradually. Those activities which suggest group work may also be managed as whole class activities.

Teaching songs

We hope that teachers will lead the singing with their own voices, particularly with younger children. But in all instances we have assumed that the teacher will use the CD.

If you feel confident, teach yourself a song using the CD and then teach it to the children.

To rehearse songs with your class without the CD, you might:
- sing the melody without the words, to lah or dee;
- chant the rhythm of the words;
- sing the song line by line for the children to copy.

Teachers' videoclips

There are fifteen videoclips on the CD-ROM that demonstrate useful teaching techniques to use in class music lessons.

Clip	Contents
T 1	The song – Nanuma
T 2	Teaching a song line by line
T 3	Starting together: speed and starting note
T 4	Pitching the starting note
T 5	Discussing phrases
T 6	Clapping the rhythm of a phrase
T 7	Demonstrating pitch with hand
T 8	Internalising
T 9	Teaching a round
T 10	Playing by ear
T 11	Teaching an accompaniment
T 12	Singing a round in two parts
T 13	Discussing performance techniques
T 14	The performance
T 15	Appraising

Ongoing skills

'Ongoing skills' are identified by the QCA scheme of work as those skills which need to be continually developed and revisited. This is in addition to the activities in the six units. The QCA suggests that learning may take place as the opportunity arises throughout the school week, eg in short 5-minute sessions.

Music Express does not include a separate Ongoing skills unit, but addresses the skills throughout its activities. When using *Music Express* as a scheme, you will be fulfilling the learning objectives and outcomes of the QCA Ongoing skills unit.

If you teach music in one weekly lesson, as opposed to three shorter lessons, you may like to select activities from *Music Express* for supplementary 5-minute activities. By doing this, you will reinforce more regularly the development of the musical skills identified by the QCA.

Extension and future learning

A & C Black website

Music Express provides all the resources you will need for teaching a year of music. We hope, however, that you will use other songs and activities to ring the changes in subsequent years or to link with other National Curriculum subjects.

The website www.acblack.com/musicexpress lists the *Music Express* activities that were drawn from or inspired by other A & C Black books, and links to other books that will supplement the activities in *Music Express.*

1st Cyclic patterns
Exploring rhythm and pulse

AFRICAN GREETINGS

1 **Transfer speech patterns onto drums and use the rhythms as starting points for improvisation**

- Explain that speech patterns in all languages are rhythmic. Demonstrate this by saying a short phrase then tapping its natural speech rhythm on a hand drum, eg

Speech: What's	for	din-ner	to-day?
Drum: 🛢	🛢🛢🛢		🛢 🛢

Invite individuals to demonstrate other short phrases in this way.

- All listen to track 1 and observe how the African drummer taps the rhythm of the words he is chanting on his drum and then decorates and embellishes the rhythm through improvisation.

Explain that the drummer is performing on the djembe – show the children the picture on the CD-ROM. Notice the bells round the man's right ankle. Explain that some djembe players tap their foot to keep time as they play, and wear ankle bells to hear the beat.

- All mark a steady beat, tapping fingertips on knees. Invite individuals in turn to chant and tap the rhythm of a short speech pattern on a hand drum in time with the beat, and then decorate and embellish the rhythm through improvisation.

Background information

- Africa is famous for its rich musical culture, particularly drumming. Drums were originally a vital form of communication in Africa, carrying messages from village to village.

- In track 1 the drummer is speaking in Mandinka. He is chanting about a hunter hunting for food.

- In track 4, the first greeting is in Mandinka, a language spoken in many West African countries, eg Mali, Guinea, Guinea Bissau, Gambia and Senegal. The second greeting is in Wolof – the national language of Senegal. Both greetings and responses mean: 'How are you doing?' – 'I'm doing fine.'

Teaching tips

- Pulse and beat are often used synonymously. Both refer to the regular heart beat of the music.

- You will need a large area for performing the game.

- Encourage as many children as possible to be leader.

- It might be helpful to count the four beats out loud until the game is established.

- To make the game easier, clap the beat at a slower tempo.

  Tempo – the speed at which music is performed.

  Cyclic pattern – a melodic or rhythmic pattern that repeats itself over and over again.

3 **Combine the beat, rhythm and tempo in a performance of Cyclic greetings**

- Divide the class into groups of six to rehearse Cyclic greetings following the instructions on the photocopiable.

Each group explores ways of alternating and combining the two call and response rhythms, and rehearses performing in time with each other at a suitable tempo. (Encourage the members of each group to swap parts regularly to give everyone the opportunity to play the rhythms.)

- Each group performs their Cyclic greetings to the class.

2 **Perform two African greetings as a call and response accompanied by body percussion**

- All clap the beat in time with track 2, marking the first of every four claps with a stamp. Continue this as you all join in with the following call and response (track 3):

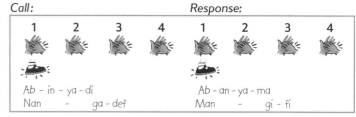

Call:				Response:			
1	2	3	4	1	2	3	4
Ab - in - ya - di		ga - def		Ab - an - ya - ma		gi - fi	
Nan				Man			

(You will hear each call and response four times.)

Join in with track 4, answering the calls with the correct response in the four-beat gap provided.

- All stand in a circle to play this rhythmic greeting game:

  – set the tempo by all clapping the beat and stamping on the first of every four beats as before (without using the CD);

  – appoint a leader to chant either of the calls (starting on a stamped beat);

  – the class chant the response starting on the next stamped beat;

  – the leader chants one of the calls again (on the next stamped beat) and the class respond...

- Play the game again, with the leader tapping the rhythm of the chosen call on a hand drum instead of chanting. (The class chant the appropriate response as before).

- Invite members of the class to tap the rhythm of the response on hand drums instead of chanting. Discuss what the class notice about the rhythm of each call and its response. (The rhythm of each call and its response is the same.)

- Play the game a third time, using only one of the greetings and only tapping the rhythm of the words. Notice that the same rhythm is repeated over and over. Explain that this is called a cyclic pattern.

Cyclic greetings

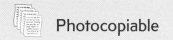

1	2	3	4	1	2	3	4

Player 1: *set the tempo by clapping the beat.*

Player 2: mark the first of every four beats throughout to indicate the beginning of each cycle:

Player 3: tap the rhythm of the call 'Ab in ya di' on a hand drum or djembe:

Player 4: tap the rhythm of the response 'Ab an ya ma' on a hand drum or djembe:

Player 5: tap the rhythm of the call 'Nan ga def' on a different untuned percussion instrument:

Player 6: tap the rhythm of the response 'Man gi fi' on the same untuned percussion instrument:

INSTRUCTIONS

Players 1 and 2 play throughout.
Each of the greeting pairs (players 3-4 and 5-6) take turns performing repetitions of their call and response.
Decide how many repetitions of each call and response to perform before swapping to the other.
See if you can perform both calls and responses at the same time.

AN AFRICAN CYCLIC PATTERN

1 Learn about African percussion instruments

- Listen to track 5, all tapping the beat using fingertips on knees.

- Listen again and discuss which instruments are being played. *(The higher-pitched drum is the djembe, and the performer is tapping his foot to mark the beat with ankle bells. There is also a deeper-sounding drum playing and a hollow-sounding bell.)*

  Explain that the deep-sounding drum is the djun djun, and that the djun djun player is also playing the bell. Show the children the picture on the CD-ROM.

- Explain that musicians in Africa make their own instruments using materials found locally, eg drum shells may be carved out of wood and covered with animal skins.

- Explain that children in Africa also make their own simple instruments to play, eg shaking pods of seeds or threading bottle tops on elastic to make wrist or ankle bracelets to wear when they dance.

- Listen to track 5 and ask the children if they hear any cyclic patterns. *(Both drummers play cyclic patterns, but the djun djun cyclic pattern is the most noticeable because it continues throughout. The djembe player performs improvisations as well as cyclic patterns.)*

Background information

- Djembe drumming is extremely popular all over West Africa, and indeed the rest of the world, though it originated in Mali.

- The djun djun player uses his right hand to beat the drum (using a stick), and plays the bell with his left hand either by holding it and tapping it with a metal thumb ring, or by attaching the bell to the top of the drum and tapping it with a beater.

- Larger drums are usually covered with cow skins and smaller drums with goat skins. Goat skins are very popular because goats are such 'talkative' animals. Their skin is therefore considered to help the drummers communicate. Other local materials used to make instruments include bamboo, calabash, fishing cord, etc.

Teaching tips

- You will need a large space to rehearse the djun djun cyclic pattern.

- Notice that the slower track marks the beats and the half beats:
  1 + 2 + 3 + 4 +
  whereas the faster track only marks the four main beats:
  1 2 3 4.

- Notice that the second clap of the djun djun cyclic pattern is more difficult to place correctly because it falls between beats.

- Encourage children who make a mistake to join in again on the next strong beat *(beat 1)*.

- Take regular turns to perform the beat or the cyclic pattern.

2 Learn the djun djun cyclic pattern

- Listen to the djun djun cyclic pattern performed slowly with the beat *(track 6)*. All join in marking the beat, tapping fingertips on knees. Listen to the cyclic pattern to get a feel for the rhythm.

- Stand in a circle to rehearse the djun djun cyclic pattern slowly with the CD. Divide the class in half:
  - one half steps on the spot to mark the beat, accenting the first of every four beats with a louder stamp;
  - the other half claps the djun djun cyclic pattern.

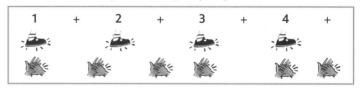

- When the class is confident performing at the slow tempo of track 6, rehearse with track 7 which is faster.

  (Confident children may like to perform the cyclic pattern on a hand drum instead of clapping.)

3 Rehearse the djun djun cyclic pattern with the bell cyclic pattern

- All listen to the cyclic pattern played by the bell *(track 8)*, and notice that it has a very similar rhythm to the djun djun cyclic pattern *(there is no tap on the first and third beat and there is an extra tap between the third and fourth beats, but otherwise it is the same)*:

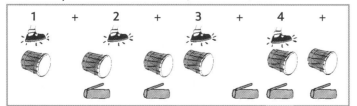

All practise tapping the bell rhythm slowly using track 9, and then up to speed with track 8.

- Divide into small groups to practise the beat, djun djun and bell cyclic patterns.

WHAT'S THE CUE?

1 Revise the djun djun and bell cyclic patterns and learn the cue

- Revise the cyclic patterns learnt in lesson 2: standing in a circle, one group marks the beat by stepping on the spot, another group claps the djun djun cyclic pattern, and a third group adds the bell cyclic pattern. (*Use tracks 5-9 for support if necessary.*)

- Listen again to track 5 to notice the rhythmic signal played on the djembe at the beginning and end of the piece.

  Explain that this is known as a 'cue'. It is played by the lead drummer (in this case the djembe player) to set the tempo and signal the beginning and end to the other players.
  (*Explain that the djembe player also plays the cue at other times during the piece to signal for other changes to occur.*)

- Learn to play the cue using track 10 (*the cue is played several times slowly; after each repetition the children copy*). Repeat this until everyone is confident.

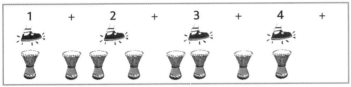

- When everyone is confident performing the cue at the slower tempo, join in with the faster tempo (*track 11*).

Background information

- Only one djembe player and one djun djun player are heard on this recording; typically there might be fifteen or more drummers and at least that many dancers. The performers are lead by the cues of the lead drummer, who also energises the music through exciting improvisations.

- The djembe drummers in the group might have several cyclic patterns to play and the dancers perform a number of repeated movements. When the leader plays the cue during the music the drummers and dancers know this is signalling them to change their pattern or movement. The final cue signals the last repetition of the cyclic patterns and all stop together.

- The djun djun cyclic pattern, played continuously throughout, helps to hold the group together, keeping the tempo steady at all times, hence it is sometimes referred to as the 'heart beat'.

Teaching tips

- Notice that the slower track marks the beats and the half beats: 1 + 2 + 3 + 4 + whereas the faster track only marks the four main beats: 1 2 3 4.

- The third and fourth claps of the cue fall before and after the second beat, not on it.

- Encourage more confident children to use hand drums instead of clapping.

- When everyone is confident starting and stopping the djun djun cyclic pattern following the cue, rehearse the bell cyclic pattern in the same way.

- Count the beat out loud as you practise.

2 Rehearse starting and stopping the djun djun cyclic pattern following the cue

- All listen to track 12 and join in marking the beat by stepping on the spot. All accent the first of every four beats with a louder stamp.

  Invite an individual to clap the rhythm of the djun djun cyclic pattern in time with the beat, starting on a strong beat (*beat 1*).

- Listen to track 13 to hear how the djun djun begins its cyclic pattern on the next strong beat after the first cue. All practise this with track 12. (*Restart the track several times to rehearse beginning the cyclic pattern on the strong beat.*)

- Once the class is confident starting the cyclic pattern correctly, all continue repeating the pattern with track 12 until the cue to finish. When the cue is played, all complete the cyclic pattern and finish with one extra beat in time with the cue (*as in tracks 5 and 13*).

- Invite volunteers to lead the class by performing the cue instead of using the CD.

3 Learn African dance movements to perform with the cyclic patterns

- Explain that African drumming pieces always accompany dancing. Use the *African dance* photocopiable and videoclips 1–3 to learn three traditional dance movements.

  Practise each dance movement individually with track 13, and then one after the other following the cue's signal (*as demonstrated on videoclip 4*).

- Appoint an individual to perform the cue (*alternatively use track 14 which gives four cues*), a small group to perform each of the djun djun and bell cyclic patterns throughout, and a group to perform the dance movements. Rehearse the following (*all agree the tempo before beginning*):

  – a first cue is given then all performers start (*dancers perform their first move*);

  – a second cue is given and the dancers change to their second move;

  – a third cue is given and the dancers change to their third move;

  – a fourth cue signals the final repeat of the cyclic patterns and all stop together.

African dance

Dance movement 1

Step right with right hand out to side.

Bring left foot to join right.

Step right again.

Bring left foot to join right.

Step left with left hand out to side.

Bring right foot to join left.

Step left again.

Bring right foot to join left.

| 1 | + | 2 | + | 3 | + | 4 | + |

Dance movement 2

Step forwards on right foot with right hand out in front (palm facing down).

Step on the spot with left foot.

Step back with the right foot with arm back over head.

Step on the spot with the left foot again.

Repeat.

| 1 | + | 2 | + | 3 | + | 4 | + |

Dance movement 3

Point right foot diagonally forwards and lean with both arms over right leg (palms facing down).

Bring right foot and both arms halfway back.

Point and lean diagonally forwards with the right foot and both arms again.

Step back with right foot and bring arms back in.

Do the same to the left.

| 1 | + | 2 | + | 3 | + | 4 | + |

IMPROVISATION

1 Rehearse ways of altering and embellishing rhythms

- Revise the patterns learnt in lessons 2 and 3. All step on the spot to set the beat, and invite individuals to demonstrate in turn the djun djun cyclic pattern, the bell cyclic pattern and the djembe's cue using hand drums.

- All listen again to track 5, and notice what the djembe plays throughout, other than the cue. *(The djembe player embellishes different rhythm patterns through improvisation.)*

- Explain that the djembe player in this recording is the leader and that there would normally be many other djembe players performing accompanying cyclic patterns whilst the leader improvised.

- Invite individuals to take turns exploring simple rhythm patterns on a hand drum in the following way:

  - the class sets a steady beat, all tapping fingertips on knees;

  - the chosen individual chooses a very simple rhythm that lasts four beats *(the rhythm could be a simple speech rhythm, eg 'abinyadi' or 'nangadef')*;

  - the individual performs the simple rhythm several times to feel how it fits with the beat;

  - gradually the player makes some simple changes to the rhythm *(eg adding extra taps on the drum, taking some away ...)*;

  - encourage individuals to make the rhythm more complicated as they gain confidence *(always making sure they keep in time with the class beat).*

  (Listen to track 1 again to give the children further inspiration.)

> **Teaching tips**
> - If anyone finds it difficult to keep more complex rhythms in time with the beat, they should revert to simpler patterns.
> - The instruments suggested may be replaced by other untuned percussion instruments if resources are limited.

> **Background information**
> - When there is a group of djembe players performing, one will be the leader.
> - The leader performs the cues to signal changes to the other players and then improvises over the cyclic patterns.
>   *(Note that this unit divides the role of playing the cue and improvising between two children to make it easier, but some children may be capable of doing both.)*
> - The other djembe players perform a series of accompanying cyclic patterns which they change following the leader's cues.

2 Take turns improvising over the djun djun and bell cyclic patterns

- Divide the class into groups. Each group will need someone to:

  - tap the beat quietly throughout and play the cues to start and stop on a djembe or hand drum;

  - play the djun djun cyclic pattern throughout on a djun djun or other deeper-sounding drum;

  - play the bell cyclic pattern throughout on a cowbell or agogo bell;

  - improvise rhythm patterns on a djembe or hand drum.

Explain that the cyclic patterns and the improvisation should start on the first strong beat after the cue, and that everyone should finish together after the second cue with one last beat.

Encourage those improvising to be spontaneous. Explain that improvisation is made up on the spot, not rehearsed.
(The members of each group should swap roles at intervals to try each part.)

3 Record and appraise group performances of the cue, cyclic patterns and solo improvisations

- Make a recording of each group performing the cue, djun djun and bell cyclic patterns while someone improvises.

- Listen to each recording and discuss the overall effect, including:

  - whether everyone started at the right time after the cue;

  - whether the performers kept in time with each other;

  - whether everyone finished together after the cue;

  - whether the improvisations were interesting.

DEGU DEGU DEGU

1 **Learn the song, *Degu degu degu***

- Listen to the song *Degu degu degu* (track 15) accompanied by the djembe drum, and by the the djun djun and bell cyclic patterns. It is sung in Bambara.

- Teach the song using tracks 16-17 (track 16 is performed very slowly to help the children learn the words and track 17 is faster for the children to practise performing the song rhythmically up to speed).

Degu degu degu, degu saramah,
Bayeh krusi badung kasentere dokang, baynah fahradi.

(*Write the words of the song on the board for initial rehearsals, but sing it from memory thereafter.*)

- When everyone is confident singing the song up to speed, invite a group to accompany the singing with the djun djun and bell cyclic patterns.

Background information

- The Bambara are the largest tribe in Mali and thus Bambara is the most widely spoken of the indigenous languages. Bambara is also related to the Mandinka language (*see lesson 1*). The official language in Mali is French, though usually only those living in urban areas who have been to school will speak it.

- *Degu degu degu* is a fun song about a dad wearing a pair of trousers that are too big and which need a belt to hold them up.

Teaching tips

- The term polyrhythm is used when more than one rhythm pattern is played at the same time.
- Track 14 provides four cues and the steady beat.

3 **Perform the cue, djun djun and bell patterns with the new cyclic patterns**

- Repeat the performance in activity 2, without the backing track:

  - a confident individual gives the four cues on a hand drum and taps the steady beat throughout;

  - one group performs the djun djun cyclic pattern throughout;

  - a second group performs the bell cyclic pattern throughout;

  - three other groups each perform one of the cyclic patterns from activity 2 on hand drums, starting one after the other following the cues (*as rehearsed in activity 2*);

  - after the fourth cue, everyone stops together.

Rehearse this until everyone is confident performing their part.

- Record a performance. Listen back and discuss:

  - how well everyone performed their parts in time together;

  - whether all parts could be heard clearly.

2 **Use song lyrics to generate new rhythms for cyclic patterns**

- Remind the children that African drumming pieces would normally include a group of djembe players. The group would accompany the dancers with different rhythms repeated as cyclic patterns and changing in response to the cues.

- Invite the children to suggest rhythms from the lyrics of the song *Degu degu degu* which might be repeated as a cyclic pattern, eg

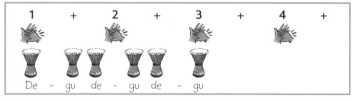

Invite a small group to repeat this rhythm over and over on hand drums using track 14 as a backing track.
(*As in other activities, the group should start this new cyclic pattern on the first strong beat after the cue.*)

- As a class, explore other rhythms on hand drums to rehearse as cyclic patterns with track 14.
(*Let as many children as possible play new cyclic patterns with the backing track.*)

- Choose three new cyclic patterns and allocate a group to perform each on hand drums with track 14:

  - group one starts their cyclic pattern after the first cue;

  - group two joins in, starting their cyclic pattern after the second cue;

  - group three joins in, starting their cyclic pattern after the third cue;

  - all finish their cycle and play one last beat on their drums after the fourth cue.

CYCLIC PERFORMANCE

1 Plan African drumming group performances

- Divide the class into groups and ask them to plan and rehearse a drumming performance. Their performance must include the beat and cue, the djun djun and bell cyclic patterns and may also include any of the following:

    - dance movements;

    - the song;

    - improvisation;

    - one or more additional cyclic patterns using a rhythm developed from the greetings *(Lesson 1)* or from the song *(Lesson 5)*.

    (If possible, encourage the children to use: djembes or hand drums for the cue and additional cyclic patterns; djun djuns or other deeper-sounding drums for the djun djun cyclic pattern; a cow bell or agogo bell for the bell cyclic pattern.)

- Each group plans their performance and begins to rehearse their ideas.

Teaching tips

- Make accessible videoclips 1–4 and the *African dances* photocopiable so the children can revise the dance movements learnt in lesson 3.

- You will need to have available as many drums and cowbells/agogo bells as possible. If resources are limited, groups may rehearse by clapping their patterns and taking turns using the available instruments.

- Circulate, monitor progress and assist as necessary.

- Encourage groups to plan their performances according to how confident they feel. Some groups may perform the beat, cue, djun djun and bell cyclic patterns only, whereas others might choose to include extra cyclic patterns, improvisation and dancing.

2 Rehearse group performances

- Each group rehearses their performance. Remind them to think about:

    - performing in time with the beat;

    - starting cyclic patterns on the next strong beat after the cue;

    - all finishing the cyclic patterns after the final cue with a final beat on the drums.

3 Appraise the group African drumming performances

- Record or video each group's performance, and invite members of the class to give both positive comments and constructive criticism to each group.

- Once all groups have performed, discuss how the performances varied and what the children have learnt about West African drumming.

IT'S A ROUND

1 Play *Round game*

- All watch the videoclip of *Round game* and notice what is happening. Play the game yourselves:

  – all sit on chairs in a circle with legs either crossed or uncrossed;

  – one child is chosen to be the starting point of the circle;

  – in unison, all say out loud to a steady tempo the order of the crossed and uncrossed legs, going round the circle clockwise, eg 'uncrossed, crossed, crossed, uncrossed ...'

  – in unison, clap the pattern instead of saying it:

  – divide the class in half to perform the round: half the class starts clapping the pattern; the second half begins when the first has clapped four sets of crossed or uncrossed legs.

Teaching tip

- As a visual aid, point out that one foot on the ground represents one clap, two feet on the group represents two claps.

Teaching tips

- Unison means that everyone performs the same thing at the same time.

- A round is a piece of music in which two or more performers or groups start one after the other. As each performer reaches the end of the music, they start again – the music going round and round – hence the name.

- The entry points of a round are those points in the music when the next performer may begin. Rounds may have two or more entry points, making them two-part, three-part, or four-part rounds, and so on. But any round may be performed by as few as two performers.

2 Learn *The human drum kit*

- Listen to the performance of the chant, *The human drum kit*, on track 18 and discuss how the verse and chorus differ. *(The verse is a unison chant, the chorus is a four-part round.)*

- Teach the verse and chorus in unison using track 19.

Vs Are you ready? (click, click) 'cause you're in for a treat,
Are you ready (click, click) with your fingers and feet?
Are you ready? (click, click) can you feel the beat?
We are the human drum kit!

Ch 1 (Stamp, stamp!) goes the big bass drum, now
2 Listen to the hi hat, (ch ch ch ch).
3 Snares go (clap clap, clap clap), followed by a
4 Crash on the cymbals, (sh._____)

3 Perform *The human drum kit* as a round

- Give everyone the *Round drum kit* photocopiable and perform the chorus as a round. Divide into two groups. When the first group reaches the entry point at the beginning of the second line, the other begins. *(An asterisk marks the entry point, but the children may also need a signal from you to help them enter correctly.)*

- When the children feel confident, divide into four groups and practise the chorus as a four-part round. Use track 18 to remind the class how the four parts sound together.

- Record a complete performance of *The human drum kit* – chant the verse in unison followed by the chorus as a round.

- Listen to the recording, noticing whether the groups were able to keep in time together. Ask how the performance might be improved *(eg it may help if one person taps a steady beat on a cowbell).*

Teaching tips

- Invite a drum kit player to accompany the round.

- Try saying the words of the chorus silently, making only the sound effects out loud.

Round drum Kit

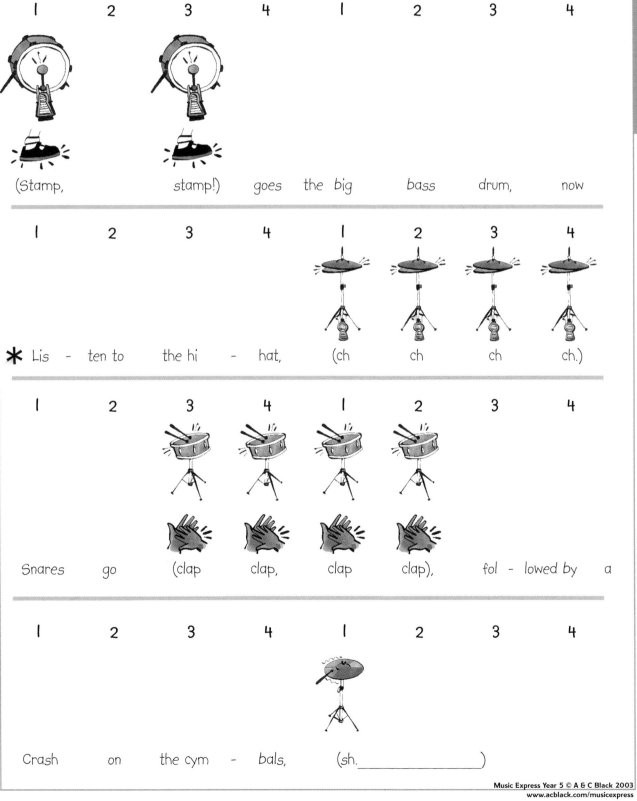
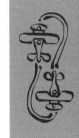

1	2	3	4	1	2	3	4

(Stamp,   stamp!)   goes   the   big   bass   drum,   now

1	2	3	4	1	2	3	4

✱ Lis - ten to   the hi   -   hat,   (ch   ch   ch   ch.)

1	2	3	4	1	2	3	4

Snares   go   (clap   clap,   clap   clap),   fol - lowed by   a

1	2	3	4	1	2	3	4

Crash   on   the cym - bals,   (sh._____)

Music Express Year 5 © A & C Black 2003
www.acblack.com/musicexpress

17

HOW DOES IT SOUND TOGETHER?

1 Revise *The human drum kit* then sing *Autumn leaves*

- Perform *The human drum kit*, Lesson 1 activity 3, and revise the terms unison, round and entry point.

- Teach the song, *Autumn leaves*, using track 20 and singing it in unison. (*Show the step-by-step descending pitch movement of each line with your hand as you sing.*)

1 Autumn leaves are
2 falling,
3 orange, red and
4 brown.
5 See them twirling
6 in the wind, and
7 floating to the
8 ground.

- When the song is secure, show the children the **Exploring pitch** photocopiable and ask them to follow the words as they listen to tracks 21 then 22. Ask the children to describe what they hear.

  - *track 21: the melody is sung once through by two voices; the second voice starts when the first reaches the third line;*

  - *track 22: the melody is sung by two voices; the second voice starts when the first reaches the second line.*

- Discuss the musical effect of the two tracks. (*The children might use words like 'clash' or 'sounds uncomfortable' in response to track 22, while they might say that track 21 'sounds comfortable' or 'doesn't clash'.*)

3 Use *Autumn leaves* to explore different combinations of pitch

- In groups or pairs, the children explore the effects of playing the melody on tuned percussion, starting one after the other at different entry points:

  - one player performs the melody as written on the **Exploring pitch** photocopiable;

  - a second player starts when the first player reaches the second line;

  - the players try again, using the third line as the entry point, then the fourth, and so on.

- As a class, listen carefully while confident pairs of children demonstrate on the tuned percussion the note combinations produced by starting at the different entry points.

- Discuss the effects created by the different note combinations, using words such as tense, tight, relaxed, comfortable. (*They might like to notice the particular effect of single pairs of notes played together.*)

- Having discovered that the different entry points produce very different note combinations, some comfortable, others tense, ask the class whether they can find an entry point which enables the song to be sung comfortably as a round.
  (*There are none. The song is not a round – all the entry points produce note combinations which clash uncomfortably when the song is repeated. To be a round, the song needs to be able to repeat without producing uncomfortable note clashes.*)

Background information

- *Autumn leaves* is not a round, but it has some of a round's characteristics: it may be sung by more than one group starting one after another – some entry points sounding more 'harmonious' than others.

- It is useful for exploring note combinations because it uses all the notes of the C major scale in descending order: C' B A G F E D C.

2 Perform *Autumn leaves* on tuned percussion

- Divide the class into groups, each with access to tuned percussion or any other available instruments with the notes C D E F G A B C'.

- Revise singing the melody of *Autumn leaves*, then ask the groups to work out the melody by ear using instruments and writing the note names on the **Exploring pitch** photocopiable.

  (*Answer: C' C' C' C', B B, A A A A, G, F F F F, E E E E, D D D D, C*)

- When each group has played and written the notes of the melody, all play the melody together in unison using track 20 to support.

Teaching tips

- The children should pass round the instruments to let as many as possible play.

- Use recorders and electronic keyboards if available, and ask children to bring in other instruments from home.

- When practising without the CD, you might like to encourage an individual to mark the beat to help everyone play in time together.

Exploring pitch

Use these notes to play the tune of **Autumn leaves** and write the names of the notes in the empty boxes.

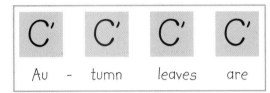

Au - tumn   leaves   are

fall - ing,

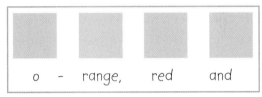

o - range,   red   and

brown.

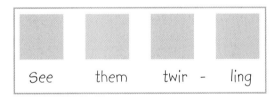

See   them   twir - ling

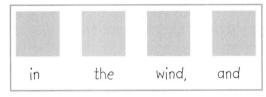

in   the   wind,   and

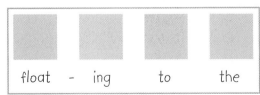

float - ing   to   the

ground.

SHALOM

1 Learn the round, *Shalom*

- Listen to *Shalom* (track 23). Explain that this is a traditional Israeli song. 'Shalom' means peace. All notice that there are four musical phrases – each line of the song being one phrase.

- Teach the song, and practise singing it in unison, marking the phrases with your hands.

  1 Shalom, my friend, shalom, my friend,
  2 Shalom, shalom.
  3 Until we meet again, my friend,
  4 Shalom, shalom.

- When the song is secure, all listen to track 24. The song is performed once in unison then as a round by four voices – all notice that the beginning of each musical phrase is an entry point, making this a four-part round.

- Practise singing the round in two, then three, then four groups

Teaching tips
- Trace an arc in the air as you sing each line of the song to show the musical phrases.
- Encourage the children to think high to help them reach the high notes.
- To give an inexperienced class practice in combining independent parts, suggest that they all sing the last line over and over again. When this is established, one half of the class starts from the beginning, while the others continue repeating the last line.

Teaching tips
- Chord – three or more notes played at the same time.
- Before revealing the notes of the chord, D F A, you might invite volunteers to find them on their instruments by listening carefully.
- Use piano, keyboard or guitar as well as tuned percussion instruments to play the accompaniment.

3 Perform *Shalom* with the chord accompaniment

- Record performances of the round with different groups accompanying with their invented patterns.
  (The accompanying group provides an introduction and ending by playing their pattern an agreed number of times before and after the song.)

- Listen to the recordings and discuss:
  – which accompaniment patterns worked well and why;
  – which instruments were most suited to the spirit and the mood of the song.

2 Add an accompaniment to *Shalom*

- Listen to track 25. Explain that the song is accompanied by a three-note chord played as a drone throughout.

- Invite a small group to join in with the accompaniment, using tuned percussion notes D F and A while the class sing.

Sha - lom, my friend, sha - lom, my friend, Sha-

(Take care that the accompaniment chord does not become louder than the singers.)

- Listen to the tuned percussion accompaniment in track 26. The accompaniment is played twice through, using the notes of the chord in a different pattern each time, eg

Sha - lom, my friend, sha - lom, my friend, Sha-

- Divide the class into small groups, each with access to the notes of the accompaniment chord – D F and A. Each group experiments to create different accompaniment patterns to perform with the song.

COME AND SING TOGETHER

1 Learn the round, *Come and sing together*

- Teach the song, *Come and sing together*, in unison using track 27. (*Ask the class to notice the dance-like mood and strong dancing beat.*)

1 If you'd dance, then (2) you must have
Boots of shining leather.
Money in your pocket book,
In your cap a feather.
But if you would sing with me,
You don't need a cent, you see, so
Come and sing together!
If you'd dance, then you must have
Boots of shining leather.

- Listen to *Come and sing together* performed as a round (*track 28*). What do the children notice about the round and the entry point? (*This is a two-part round and the entry point comes very near to the beginning of the first phrase.*) Ask which word marks the entry point ('*you*').

- When the class is confident singing the song in unison, divide into two groups and sing the song as a round.

Teaching tips

- The class may have difficulty with:

  - keeping in time with each other: help them by tapping a steady beat on a woodblock, and asking them to tap or lightly clap the beat with you as they sing;

  - coming in at the correct entry point: help them by playing the beginning of track 28 several times to familiarise them with the entry point; when singing the round, signal the entry point clearly.

Background information

- *Come and sing together* is a traditional Hungarian folk song.

2 Add an accompaniment to the round

- All listen to the accompaniment of the song in track 29 (*slower version*), and follow it on the *Dancing boots* photocopiable. Ask the children if the accompaniment chord is the same all through or if it changes. (*It changes.*)

- Explain that this song uses two different chords:

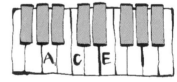 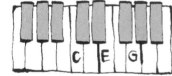

- Invite a small group to join in playing the chord accompaniment with track 29, using keyboards, piano or tuned percussion.
- When this is secure, the group may accompany the rest of the class singing the song as a two-part round. When all are confident, perform the song at the faster tempo of tracks 27/28.
  (*Encourage those playing the chords to make a bright, joyous sound.*)
- Invite volunteers to play a steady beat on untuned percussion instruments as part of the accompaniment (*this might be a fast or slow steady beat, as demonstrated on the CD*).

3 Perform *Come and sing together* with the accompaniment

- Perform the song in the following way:
  - decide on a suitable introduction;
  - sing the song in unison with the chord accompaniment and slow steady beat;
  - repeat it twice as a round, once with the chord accompaniment, adding the fast steady beat during the last repeat.

  (*Decide who will play the chords, who will play the steady beats and who will sing.*)

- Record the performance, then listen back to discuss:
  - whether it creates a dance-like mood;
  - whether there is a good balance between song and accompaniment.

Dancing boots

| 1 | 2 | 1 | 2 | 1 | 2 | 1 | 2 |

E C A — **E C A** — **E C A** — **E C A**

If you'd dance, then you must have   Boots of shi - ning lea – ther.

E C A — **E C A** — **E C A** — **E C A**

Mo - ney in your po - cket book,   In your cap a fea – ther.

G E C — **G E C** — **G E C** — **G E C**

But if you would   sing with me,

G E C — **G E C** — **G E C** — **G E C**

You don't need a   cent, you see. so

E C A — **E C A** — **E C A** — **E C A**

Come and sing to - ge - ther!   If you'd dance, then you must have

E C A — **E C A**

Boots of shi - ning lea - ther.

CALYPSO

1 Learn a calypso rhythm pattern

- Listen to track 30. The bongos are playing a calypso rhythm. Listen again and join in with the words 'carnival carnival dancing'.

- Join in again, all tapping the rhythm on knees:

1	2	3	1	2	3	1	2
RH	LH	LH	RH	LH	LH	RH	LH
Car	- ni	- val	car	- ni	- val	dan	- cing,

- When everyone is confident tapping this pattern, divide the class into two groups. One group taps the rhythm practised and the other only the right hand taps – the claves rhythm on track 30.

- Repeat the activity with some of the first group playing their pattern on bongos and some of the other group playing the right hand pattern on claves:

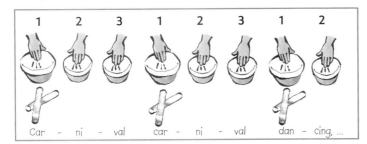

| 1 | 2 | 3 | 1 | 2 | 3 | 1 | 2 |

Car – ni – val   car – ni – val   dan – cing, ...

Teaching tips

- Count the beats to begin with, but encourage the children to feel the rhythm by letting them move to the dance-like rhythm as they play and sing.

2 Learn the round, *Calypso*

- Teach the song in unison using track 31:

1 Anytime you need a calypso, here is what you must do.
2 First of all you need a rhythm, so shake a little,
    shake a little, shake a little shaker, and you
3 Bang a drum and you sing and strum and then there's
    a calypso for you.

Background information

- *Calypso* is an easy relaxed rhythm pattern associated with Trinidad. It has eight half beats to the bar but a stress is laid on beats 1, 4 and 7 which is shown above as:

  1 2 3 1 2 3 1 2
  (**1** 2 3 **4** 5 6 **7** 8)

- All listen to *Calypso* performed on track 32 and notice how it is organised. (*It is sung once in unison and then twice as a round. It is a three-part round with entry points on the words 'first' and 'bang'.*)

- Practise singing the song as a three-part round.

3 Perform *Calypso* as a round with accompaniments

- Practise singing *Calypso* in unison with a small group accompanying with the percussion parts from activity 1. (*Use track 31 as a support if required*).

- All listen to the tuned percussion part which can also be heard on track 31. Invite a volunteer to clap the rhythm:

| 1 | 2 | 3 | 1 | 2 | 3 | 1 | 2 | 1 | 2 | 3 | 1 | 2 | 3 | 1 | 2 ... |

- Invite an individual to play the tuned percussion part by ear using the notes C F G. (*If needed, the answer is written on the Performing calypso photocopiable.*)

- Practise performing *Calypso* in unison and as a round with the untuned and tuned percussion accompaniments.

Performing calypso

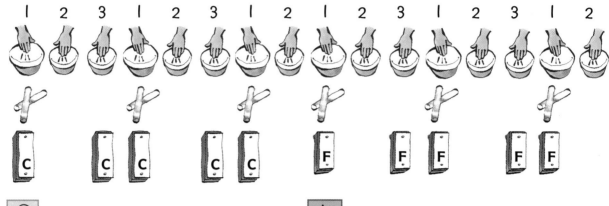

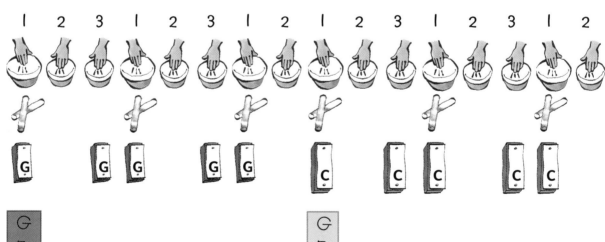

CALYPSO PERFORMANCE

1 Revise the song, *Calypso*

- Revise singing *Calypso* in three groups with the tuned and untuned percussion accompaniments from the previous lesson.

- Listen to track 31, following the bass xylophone, bongos and claves parts on the *Performing calypso* photocopiable.

- Listen again to track 31 and notice the chords played on glockenspiel. Listen again and follow the chords on the photocopiable.

- Invite a small group to play the chords, while the others sing the song and play the other percussion parts.
  (They will need the notes C D E F G' A' on tuned percussion, or a keyboard.)

Teaching tips

- If possible give the group playing the chords some opportunity to rehearse away from the class.

2 Rehearse *Calypso* 33

- Rehearse the song with a small group playing the chords as the class sings.

  Decide who will perform which instrumental part and who will sing.

- Practise the song in the structure performed on track 32, with or without backing track 33:

  – instrumental introduction (*chords and claves once through as on the photocopiable, then a second time through adding the melodic ostinato*);

  – song (*once in unison adding the bongos to the accompaniment*);

  – round (*twice through in three groups with all the accompaniment parts*);

  – ending (accompaniment parts played once through).

- Think about expression, particularly dynamics. Ask where in the performance you might get quieter or louder for effect.
  (For example, the second line 'so shake a little shake a little shake a little shaker' might start quietly and gradually get louder to reach the word 'Bang'.)

- Invite individuals to take turns listening to the rehearsal and encourage them to advise on the balance between all the parts. They should check that the accompaniment does not drown out the singing, and offer suggestions for improvement.

Teaching tips

- Encourage strong energetic singing.
- Ask the children to stand up to rehearse and perform their singing.

3 Perform Calypso

- Perform *Calypso* as practised in activity 2. If possible **video** and/or **record** the performance as a record of your achievement.

Journey into space
Exploring sound sources

CLUSTERS 1

1 Listen to the use of clusters in *Atmosphères*

- Ask the children to listen to, and then describe the sounds they hear in the extract from *Atmosphères*.
  (Lots of notes close together in pitch, all played at the same time and sustained.)

- Explain that a collection of closely-pitched notes all played at once is called a cluster. Demonstrate clusters on a piano or electronic keyboard by sounding sets of adjacent notes together *(black, white or a mixture)*.

- Listen to the extract of *Atmosphères* again. Ask the children what happens to the cluster of notes.
  (The notes of the cluster are held for a long time. Notes gradually leave the cluster and new notes join to form continuously changing clusters which become higher and higher in pitch.)

- Ask the class whether the music is acoustic (are non-electric instruments such as violins playing?) – or are the sounds produced electronically? *(The music is acoustic – instruments are playing.)*

- Discuss the composer's use of the elements of music in this piece *(see Teaching tips below)*.

Background information

- *Atmosphères* was composed in 1961 by the Hungarian composer, György Ligeti (1923–). Ligeti's use of clusters as a composing technique is fundamental to his work.

- Ligeti wrote this piece for a large orchestra, but it was inspired by the innovative electronic sounds he was encountering through his work in a music studio.

Teaching tips

- Think about the following when discussing how Ligeti uses the elements of music in *Atmosphères*:

  duration – notes are sustained for a long time; there is no sense of rhythm or steady beat;

  tempo – there is no beat, but there is an impression of the music moving very slowly;

  texture – many different instruments are playing simultaneously and overlapping; the texture grows from single notes to thick clusters and back again;

  timbre – the individual sounds of instruments merge into each other and form constantly changing new timbres;

  dynamics – the music starts very quietly but there are dramatic increases and decreases in volume;

  pitch – this changes very slowly as the clusters get gradually higher and higher in pitch.

2 Create and perform clusters on instruments

- Bring together a range of tuned instruments which can produce sustained sounds, eg keyboard, recorders *(children might bring in instruments they are learning, eg violin or flute)*.

  Select a group of children to play. The group finds a set of adjacent notes, one note per player, and practises combining them. *(Videoclip 6 demonstrates combining notes in this way to make clusters.)*

- Choose a conductor to try these ideas:

  – signal each player to start playing one by one, then drop out one by one;

  – signal everyone to play together immediately;

  – divide the group into three sections and alternate between them to create an effect of overlapping clusters;

  – vary the dynamics by signalling an increase in volume using arm movement, or increasing the number of players;

  – signal the instruments to begin playing in sequence from the lowest-sounding through to the highest-sounding.

- As a class assess the effects produced by the group, comparing them to the effects in *Atmosphères*.

  Repeat the activity with a different conductor and different children playing instruments.

3 Create clusters using voices

- Explore clusters with voices in the following ways *(these are demonstrated on videoclip 7)*:

  – all sing the same note together, then invite a conductor to direct individuals to move the pitch of their note a little higher or lower to create a cluster;

  – one child sings a note and holds it continuously, then a conductor invites individuals to join in, singing a note that will clash with the one being sung. Gradually more and more children are included.

  Give several children opportunities to conduct. The conductor experiments with directing individuals or the entire group to get louder or quieter, or to change the pitch of individual notes. *(Everyone takes a breath whenever they need to. They should take care to find the same note again after the breath.)*

CLUSTERS 2

1 Compare the use of clusters in *Atmosphères* and *Départ*

- Listen again to *Atmosphères* (track 34) and ask the class to recap how the composer uses clusters (see Lesson 1 activity 1).

- Listen to *Départ* (track 35). Ask the children how this composition differs from *Atmosphères*, eg

  - duration (*there are sporadic, short bursts of sound; some sounds are long and sustained, others are short*);

  - tempo (*there is no steady beat, but there is an impression of the music moving quickly*);

  - texture (*single notes as well as combinations may be heard on their own and overlapping; thin and thick textures are dramatically alternated*);

  - timbre (*though performed on acoustic instruments there is no attempt to mimic electronic sounds; voices and percussion are used as well as orchestral instruments; timbre is used to create splashes of musical colour*);

  - dynamics (*the music changes volume suddenly and dramatically, taking the listener by surprise*);

  - pitch (*there are vivid contrasts between very high and very low notes which again happen suddenly and surprisingly*).

Background information

- *Départ* was composed in 1988 by Wolfgang Rihm (born Germany, 1952).

3 Explore recording techniques and discuss how sounds change when recorded

- Record one of the activity 2 compositions: arrange the performers as before, seat the listeners behind the conductor and in the same position place a basic cassette recorder. Record the performance.

- Play the recording and ask the listeners to say what was different about the experience of hearing the performance live and hearing the recording, eg

  - they may notice sounds in the recording which they didn't notice in the live performance, and vice versa;

  - they may notice that the quality of the sound is poor (depending on the quality of the recording equipment).

- Ask the conductor and performers for their comments on the quality of the recording:

  - could the performers hear themselves clearly?

  - was the conductor happy with the balance between individual and group sounds, between loud and quiet sounds?

- If you have access to higher quality recording equipment and external microphones, repeat the activity with the aim of recording a more faithful version of the performance. You will need to consider how to position the performers and the microphones in order to capture the best quality, balance and clarity of sounds.

- Summarise together what you have learnt about making a recording.

2 Explore clusters and single sounds using voices, keyboards and other instruments

- Divide the class into vocalists, instrumentalists and listeners. Subdivide the vocal and instrumental groups further into small groups and individuals. Make available the instruments from Lesson 1.

  Ask the groups and individuals to practise their clusters and single sounds quietly, considering whether they will be:

  - short or sustained;

  - overlapping or simultaneous;

  - loud or quiet; remaining at the same volume or changing;

  The listeners move amongst the performers noting the effects.

- Each individual or small group makes a note of the key attributes of their sound on a large piece of card for everyone to see, eg

  violin - short, loud, high-pitched

  voices - sustained, tense, overlapping

- Arrange the groups and individuals in a semicircle with the descriptive cards clearly visible. Invite one of the listeners to create a composition by directing each individual and group to perform once when pointed to.

  (Repeat the activity with different conductors from the listening group. Encourage the conductors to aim to create different moods by the way they contrast or merge sounds.)

Teaching tips

- It is important that quiet sound sources are audible on the recording, but they should not be positioned so close to a microphone that they are too loud in relation to other sounds.

ATTACK AND DECAY

1 **Listen to *Stripsody* and explore the attack and decay of sounds, using voices**

- Listen to *Stripsody*. Discuss the sounds used in the piece, and invite the children to demonstrate any they remember (*'slam', 'stchk', 'stop', 'weeaa'*).

  Listen again and notice how the singer exaggerates the attack and decay of the words and sounds she makes (*eg 'slaammm', 'k-reak', 'sweeeeeeeee', 'weeaweeeee'*). Notice which words have a hard attack (*'creak'*) or soft attack (*'slam'*), and those which have a long decay (*'sweeeee'*) or short decay (*'stop'*).

- As a class, choose four words to sing in this exaggerated way (*select words which begin and end with vowels and consonants to give a contrast of attack and decay, eg – car, arm, toe, soup*).

  Divide the class into groups. Each group chooses three of the words and a selection of letters (*vowels and consonants*) from the alphabet.

- Each group explores exaggerating the words and letters. They write an order for everyone to follow, and record a performance.

Background information

- *Stripsody* was written in 1966 by Cathy Berberian (1925-1983).
- Attack refers to the start of a sound and is described in terms of hard/fast or soft/slow (eg the word 'car' has a hard attack, 'arm' – soft attack).
- Decay refers to the length of time a sound takes to die away and is described as long or short (eg cymbal clash – long decay, woodblock – short decay).

3 **Choose and perform sounds to add to *Outer space***

- Listen to the *Outer space* backing track (*track 38*) and ask the class about the sounds they hear (*electronic sounds; sounds which slowly merge in and out; a repeated echo sound throughout; sounds with soft attacks and long decays*).

  What characteristics of space does the music convey? (eg, *immense distance, emptiness, vastness, indefinite sense of time.*)

- Explain that the groups from activity 2 may use a keyboard (*and their completed photocopiables*), a set of acoustic instruments and their voices to add sounds to track 38 to enhance the effect of a space soundscape. Give the groups time and space to practice their sounds, encouraging them to use what they have learnt in previous lessons about:

  – clusters, vocal sounds, keyboard sounds, attack and decay;
  – use of musical elements (*encourage the groups to explore: the duration of their sounds; pitch or change of pitch; volume and volume changes; texture and timbre.*)

- Give each group the opportunity to practise adding their sounds to the backing track.

- Each group performs *Outer space* to the class.

- Discuss each performance, inviting members of the class to comment on the effectiveness of the soundscapes.

2 **Explore the attack and decay of keyboard sounds**

- Make and display a class list of electronic keyboard voices, eg *flute, choir, cosmic sound*. Group the voices into those which represent another musical instrument (*eg violin, human voice*), everyday sounds (*eg traffic, seashore, telephone ...*) and invented sounds (*eg fantasy, space ...*).

- All listen to track 37 which gives four different keyboard sounds played twice. As a class decide what kind of attack and decay each sound has. (*Answer: sound 1 hard attack short decay; sound 2 hard attack long decay; sound 3 soft attack short decay; sound 4 soft attack long decay.*)

- Discuss how the sounds have been electronically created, checking that the children know what is meant by synthesising and sampling (see below).

- Compare the real sound of available instruments with their keyboard sound. Discuss how well the sound has been reproduced:

  – does the electronic sound reproduce the attack of the acoustic instrument?
  – does it reproduce the decay?
  – is the sound better in one part of the keyboard than another?

- Explain that the class will be contributing to a composition called *Outer space*.

  Divide the class into small groups. Give each group turns to use a keyboard. On a copy of the *Outer space sounds* photocopiable, the group makes a note of the sounds they have found which they would like to contribute to the composition. They write the keyboard settings on the photocopiable, including any settings which alter the sound further (*eg pitch bend wheel, reverb*).

Background information

- Synthesised and sampled sounds are used widely in all kinds of music and have enabled the development of new instruments (eg keyboard, drum machine), as well as new ways of composing.
- Synthesising – the process of creating sounds electronically.
- Sampling – the process of recreating a real sound electronically and then digitally encoding it.

Outer space sounds

Find three sounds on your electronic keyboard for each section below.
Make sure you write down the keyboard settings.

Sounds with a strong attack		

Sounds with a long decay		

Our favourite sounds		

Music Express Year 5 © A & C Black 2003
www.acblack.com/musicexpress

MOON LANDING

1 Discuss moods and feelings about the first moon landing as captured in a videoclip and musical composition

- Watch the videoclip of the first moon landing (*videoclip 8*). Explain the background to the videoclip, and discuss how the astronauts might be feeling.
(Relieved to have landed safely. Excited to be the first people ever to have landed and stepped on the moon. Proud to be representing their country. Nervous of the unknown.)

- Discuss what Neil Armstrong meant when he said 'one small step for man, one giant leap for mankind'.

- Listen to *Mare tranquillitatis* (*track 39*). Explain that this is one composer's sound picture of the first moon landing.

- Listen again, and ask the children about the sounds they can hear.

(The composer uses electronic sounds and recordings of the astronauts talking. Many layers of sound are overlapped and combined. Sounds gradually change, cease, or start again.)

Background information

- The first successful moon landing was the American Apollo 11 mission which landed on the moon on 20th July, 1969. The Apollo 11 crew consisted of Neil Armstrong, Michael Collins and Edwin E. Aldrin.

- *Mare tranquillitatis* was written by Greek composer, Vangelis (born 1943). Vangelis is most widely known for the film music of *Chariots of fire*.

3 Select sound sources for *Moonscape* music

- Explain that the children are going to create group compositions – soundscapes of the moon landing. They will begin working in pairs. As a class, discuss these four parts of the soundscape:
    - the space ship;
    - an astronaut moonwalking;
    - outer space;
    - stars.

- As a class, brainstorm the characteristics of each part of the soundscape *(eg are any of the mechanical sounds of the space ship rhythmic? Is moonwalking fast, slow, jerky, smooth?)*.

Watch the videoclip of the moon landing again for inspiration.

- Divide the class into pairs, allocating a part of the soundscape to each. Ask all the pairs to consider the sound sources they might use for their part of the soundscape, eg
    - soundmakers they can create (as in *Spacescape*);
    - their voices (as explored in *Stripsody*), or the astronauts' own voices (as on Videoclip 8 and *Mare tranquilitatis*);
    - keyboard sounds (explored in Lesson 3);
    - other electronic sounds, eg computer sounds, digital watches, the sound of a radio being retuned;
    - acoustic instruments (as explored in Lesson 1);
    - a recorded background of sounds to which live sounds are added in performance (as in Lesson 3).

- Encourage each pair to keep notes of their ideas on sound sources for the next lesson.

2 Listen to *Spacescape* and discuss how everyday objects have been used as instruments

- Listen to *Spacescape* (*track 40*) then look at the *Space soundmakers* photocopiable. Explain that these were the soundmakers the composer used to create his soundscape, using very simple recording equipment in a large resonant hall.

Listen to track 41 in which the soundmakers are played in the order numbered on the photocopiable. Notice which soundmakers are used to make:
    - long/short sounds;
    - melodic/rhythmic ostinati;
    - single sounds/clusters;
    - scratchy/rustly/breathy/boomy timbres;
    - changes in pitch.

- Listen again to track 40 and discuss how the composer uses the sounds in the soundscape.

(Some are heard individually or together; some are heard repeatedly, intermittently, or only once or twice; there are melodic and rhythmic ostinati as well as arhythmic, free sounds.)

Teaching tips

- Convey to the children that any sound can be used to make music.

- Encourage them to consider creating or enhancing sounds with simple recording techniques, eg

    - interesting effects can be achieved simply by recording in a large hall or by positioning sound sources near to or far from a microphone;

    - some keyboards have a simple multi-tracking recording facility;

    - computer software for recording, combining and layering sounds is accessible on the internet (see links from the Music Express website).

Space soundmakers

1.
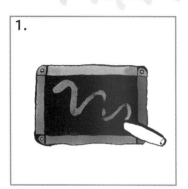
long, hissing

2.

scrape
short, bright, harsh

3.

twang...
jagged, pitch change

4.

tear
long, scratchy

5–6.

short boom/long rumble

7.

rattle
long, rustly

8.

blow...
MILK
deep, long, breathy

9.

warm, slow melody

10.

short clusters

11.

scrunch
long, crackly

Music Express Year 5 © A & C Black 2003
www.acblack.com/musicexpress

Journey into space
Exploring sound sources

MOONSCAPE

1 Begin composing the parts of *Moonscape*

- The pairs from Lesson 4 activity 3 refer to their sound source ideas and start experimenting with them to create their part of the soundscape: the space ship, an astronaut moonwalking, outer space, or stars. These will later be combined in the group composition called *Moonscape*.

- Each pair demonstrates their sounds to the class.

  Encourage those listening to give feedback on what they liked best about the effects created and to suggest ways to improve them.

- The pairs refine their compositions and make notes of what they have done for later (*eg keyboard settings, directions for playing particular sound effects, graphic notations, recorded sound, suggestions for improvement ...*).

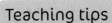

Teaching tips

- Encourage each group to discuss the overall mood they want to create, and keep this in mind while they are developing their composition.
- Make available the videoclip of the moon landing and all the recorded music for this unit as sources of inspiration, ideas and composing techniques.
- Encourage the groups to notate the structure of their composition in a graphic score, eg each part of the soundscape might be represented by a different coloured block. Extend and overlap the blocks in a visual representation of the music.

2 Combine the parts into *Moonscape* compositions

- Arrange the pairs from activity 1 into groups of four pairs each – one pair for each part of the soundscape:

  – the space ship;

  – an astronaut moonwalking;

  – outer space;

  – stars.

  Explain that the pairs will work together to layer their sounds to create a complete soundscape.

- Encourage each group to think carefully about the balance and structure of their soundscape, eg

  – are any parts of the soundscape to be present throughout?

  – if all are combined at once is the texture too thick?

  – how will the piece begin and end?

  – how will each pair know when to start and stop their sounds, or make them louder or quieter?

- The groups begin work on their compositions, discussing and rehearsing their ideas.

- At regular intervals, visit each group to listen to progress, offering guidance if required.

3 Groups share their *Moonscape* work-in-progress with the class

- Each group performs their soundscape to the class and is given constructive feedback about ways it might be improved.

MOONSCAPE RECORDING

1 **Revise *Moonscape* group compositions and make final alterations**

- Explain that the aim during the last lesson is to record a final version of each *Moonscape* composition.

- Give each group time and space to revise their work so far, encouraging them to perfect the balance between parts and timing of the performance using suggestions from previous feedback, eg

  - if they have combined pre-recorded sounds with live sounds, they will need to rehearse their sychronisation and check that the balance of volume is appropriate;

  - if their work is composed entirely of sounds played live they will need to work on their ability to perform as a group.

Teaching tips

- The class will need to be patient while each group sets up for their recording, and will then need to be silent during and at the end of the recording so that the group may assess its success.

2 **Discuss suitable recording techniques and record each group's *Moonscape***

- Each group considers the recording resources available and plans the recording of their completed soundscape, eg where to position themselves in relation to microphones. *(Remind the children of the experimentation with recording carried out in Lesson 1.)*

- Each group takes turns setting up their recording area and records a performance of their composition.

3 **Listen to and assess the *Moonscape* compositions and recordings**

- Watch the videoclip of the moon landing and then listen to each group's recording. *(It may be appropriate to play the videoclip at the same time as the recording.)*

  Discuss the effectiveness of each composition in representing the moon landing, eg

  - have the sounds been combined and used expressively?

  - have the sounds been layered effectively?

  - does the music convey an appropriate mood?

  - can the group talk about their music?

- Discuss the recordings themselves, eg;

  - how do they differ?

  - were any groups able to set their recording up with a noticeably better effect?

  - what would the groups change about their recording, if anything?

WHAT CAN WE DO?

1 Sing *Children of Africa* and investigate its purpose and context

- Listen to *Children of Africa* and discuss its social context:
  - who the original singers were (*people of South Africa during the time of apartheid*);
  - when and where it might have been performed (*by protesters on the streets of Soweto*);
  - who the audience was (*the people themselves – it is a crowd rallying song, sung to unite people*).

- Learn the song by joining in with the group singing on the CD:

Vs1 We are the children of Africa
And it's for freedom that we're fighting.
We are the children of Africa
And it's for freedom that we're fighting.

Ch A heavy load, a heavy load,
And it will take some real strength.
A heavy load, a heavy load,
And it will take some real strength.

Vs2 In Soweto they shot us down,
But we will rise up united ...

Ch A heavy load ...

3 Listen to *Nowhere else to go* and investigate its purpose and context

- Listen to *Nowhere else to go* and discuss its social context:
  - who the performer is (*a solo singer*);
  - when and where it might have been performed (*by a protest singer at a concert*);
  - who the audience is (*any gathering of people interested in the issues*).

- Ask what makes this a song for a solo singer rather than a crowd of protesters, eg
  - *it tells a personal story in a chatty, speech-like style;*
  - *the lyrics and melody are long and quite complex;*
  - *the verse lyrics contain no repetition; the chorus lyrics contain repetition but also unpredictable changes;*
  - *no phrases of the melody are exactly the same.*

- Ask what makes the song work well for its purpose, eg
  - *it is entertaining; tells a story; has a positive message that by joining together people can prevent the destruction of habitats; the melody is catchy and fun.*

- As a class, brainstorm issues the children feel strongly about and on which they would like to base a new protest song. Record the ideas in the *Songwriter's notebook* for later (CD-ROM p2).

Background information

- Songs of protest may be sung to inform, amuse and inspire an audience, or, like *Children of Africa* may be sung by the protesters themselves, often in street marches.
- Lyrics – the words of a song.

2 Investigate the structure of *Children of Africa*

- Give the class copies of page 1 from the *Songwriter's notebook*. Notice:
  - that the song structure is verse and chorus;
  - that the lyrics and melody come in pairs of phrases:

  A We are the children of Africa

  B And it's for freedom that we're fighting

  - these are repeated:

  verse A B A B chorus C D C D

- The song has a short, memorable structure. Ask the children why this suits it to its purpose as a crowd protest song, eg
  - *as soon as the lyrics and melody are heard once they are repeated, enabling everyone to join in;*
  - *the lyrics can be changed easily.*

- Ask what else makes the song work well for its purpose, eg
  - *the strong marching beat.*

- As a class, suggest alternatives for the words 'Africa', 'freedom' and 'fighting', to reflect other issues the children identify, eg

  We are the children of refugees,
  And it's our homes we are leaving.

- Sing the song with the new words, noticing any changes in mood, tempo or volume the words suggest.

Teaching tips

- Use a large format scrap book for a class *Songwriter's notebook* and paste into it the CD-ROM pages.
- Make available newspaper clippings relating to the issues the children might explore. Use them to find words and phrases which might be used in song lyrics now or later.
- Give the class plenty of encouragement to throw around ideas without worrying too much about getting things right first time.

MAKE YOUR VOICES HEARD

1 **Play the *Same or different* game to explore repetition and contrast in lyrics**

- All learn these four chant lines (*track 44*):

  A Sweeping, sweeping, sweeping the street.
  B Brush, brush, keep the beat.
  C Tap tap tappin', shuffle your feet.
  D All you gotta do is make it neat.

- Sit in a circle and practise saying line A one after another round the circle to backing track 45. Do this again, asking the children to notice the point when the repetition becomes boring for them *(this will vary)*.

- Now explain that this is a game about feeling when something needs to change, and that they will choose when to make that change. Start chanting line A round the ring to track 45. At any point, the next person in the ring can change to a different line. Each time, the person following reverts to the repeated line, and so on round.

- Explain that you are going to develop the idea of same or different further. Listen to tracks 46 and 47 and notice how the chant lines are structured (*Answer: AAAD, AABB*).

- Divide into groups of four. Each group devises a new four-line structure with two or more lines of the chant. Invite the groups to perform their work to track 45, asking the class for helpful feedback – was there an effective balance of same and different?

3 **Write a protest song as a class**

- Explain that the class has a commission to write a song. The brief is:
  - that the song is for a class protest group;
  - its audience is the protesters themselves.

- Take a vote to select one of the issues from Lesson 1 activity 3 then all play a word association game with the issue as the topic, eg:
  - you start the game by saying 'global warming', point to child one who says the first related word or phrase they think of, eg 'changing weather', child two says 'rising seas'...

- As a class formulate a lyric with eight syllables which can be chanted to a clapped steady beat, eg

1	2	3	4	1	2	3	4
War-ning	signs	of	glo -	bal	warm -	ing

- Formulate a second line together to create an ABAB structure, eg

  A Warning signs of global warming,
  B Rising seas and crashing waves,
  A Warning signs of global warming,
  B Rising seas and crashing waves.

- As a class choose two melody phrases from any one of the *Melody maker* photocopiables to provide the A and B parts of the melody (*repeat notes to accommodate any extra syllables.*)

- Together, make up lyrics for a new verse, A C A C.

- Record, play back, evaluate and improve your song as a class.

- When the class is satisfied with the results of their work, make a clean copy of the lyrics and melody in the *Songwriter's notebook* (CD-ROM page 5), and share it at an assembly, inviting audience participation.

2 **Explore repetition and contrast in melody**

- Divide the class into groups of four again and give each group a copy of the *Melody maker* photocopiable, and a set of tuned percussion notes D E F G A, or keyboard.

- As a class, listen to, sing, play and memorise the four melody phrases, which are given on track 48 and the photocopiable.

- In their groups the children explore different ways of arranging any or all of the four phrases to make an effective four-phrase melody. (*There are any number of ways of combining two or more of the phrases.*)

- They write a first draft melody on the photocopiable.

- Invite groups to play their melodies to the class for evaluation, eg
  - *is the complete melody interesting and memorable;*
  - *does it use repetition and contrast effectively.*

- The groups continue drafting ideas and finding a variety of possible melody solutions, until they settle on one they prefer. (*Make available extra copies of the photocopiable if needed.*)

Teaching tips
- Encourage the *Melody maker* groups to draft several melodies to explore what can be done with the phrases.
- For further exploration, alternative *Melody maker* phrases are given on CD-ROM pages 3-4.

Melody maker

Melody maker phrases using notes **D E F G A**

1	2	3	4	1	2	3	4
F	A	A	A	A	F	D	
A	G	F	E	F	A	F	
E	D	E	D	E	F	D	
D	F	A	A	E	F	D	

First draft

1	2	3	4	1	2	3	4

Favourite melody

1	2	3	4	1	2	3	4

MELODY MOODS

1 Listen to *Ocean of mystery* and compare it with previous song models

- Write the words on the board and teach *Ocean of mystery* using track 49:

Vs1 A big blue giant cloaks the land;
He sprays the cliffs and hugs the sand,
With a mighty roar he crashes down,
And laughs from under his foamy crown.

Ch Ocean of mystery,
Deep your secrets lie.
Ocean of mystery,
Where the seagulls fly.

Vs2 Swelling with his stormy power,
Waves as tall as any tower,
With a mighty roar he crashes down,
And laughs from under his foamy crown.

Ch Ocean of mystery ...

- Consider the song's context: who the performer might be, when and where the song might be sung, who are the audience.

- Ask the class to identify the basic difference between this song and the previous song models. (*It is descriptive and atmospheric, it evokes a sound picture of the sea, it conveys no protest message but invites us to consider the ocean environment with a sense of awe.*)

- Sing the song again and ask the class to notice:
  - which key words and phrases are stressed or repeated;
  - in what way the word rhythms differ from those of the class song (*the word rhythms in the class song are fairly close to speech; these rhythms are quite unlike speech*);
  - if the song has a marching beat (*no, it has a lilting rhythm which gives an impression of rolling waves*);
  - how the melody moves (*it is wide ranging; it rises and falls in steps and leaps like the ocean it describes*).

- On copies of CD-ROM page 6, the class handwrite the words of the song and work out the lyrics and melody structure (*CD-ROM answer sheet*).

2 Change the mood and rhythm of lyrics

- Write one phrase from the *Same or different* chant on the board, eg

  Sweeping sweeping sweeping
    the street

  All say it together to remind yourselves of the rhythm.

  Explain that the class is going to use this phrase to explore word setting further.

- Ask the class to say the phrase silently to themselves, considering how the rhythm and mood of the words can be changed. (*Help them to hear a different rhythm and mood by asking them to sing the words in their heads to the melody of Children of Africa, Ocean of mystery, or in a contemporary popular style.*)

- Invite confident volunteers to perform the phrase in the styles they have tried.

Teaching tips

- Encourage the children to think expressively, saying the lyrics to themselves in ways which:
  - reflect the moods inspired by the words: tired, energetic, sad, happy;
  - take account of when words might be performed in sustained voices, or in short, fast bursts of sound.
- Encourage them to have fun with these activities – to just have a go.

3 Compose melody lines in different moods and rhythms

- Make available keyboards or sets of tuned percussion with these notes:

  | C D E G A | F♯ G B♭ C' | D E F G A B C'D' |

- In groups of four, the children choose one set of notes. They take the phrase from activity 2 and set it to one melody line in at least three new styles of rhythm and mood, considering:
  - the effect they want to achieve: eg grand, meek, sustained, punchy, gloomy, light;
  - whether to move the melody by steps or leaps, or both;
  - which words should be emphasised on strong beats.

- Give groups frequent opportunities to share their ideas and get feedback from the class. They record their final ideas in the class *Songwriter's notebook* (*CD-ROM page 7*).

  (*If the children have difficulty getting started, it may help them to hear on track 50 how others have played with the phrase to create a number of different settings of the 'street sweeping' phrase. Notice how the words have been changed or repeated to create a new style. All the ideas are different and all are valid.*)

Songwriter
Exploring lyrics and melody

A NEW SONG COMMISSION

1 Revise what the class has learnt about songs and songwriting so far

- Revise what the class have learnt about songs and song-writing, referring to the class *Songwriter's notebook* and adding anything else the children have found out for themselves, eg

  – context: who is the singer; when and where is the song sung; who are the audience?

  – song structures: verse and chorus, call and response, verses only: and ways of labelling them, eg ABAB, etc;

  – repetition and contrast: striking a balance;

  – word-setting: eg stress, rhythm, mood;

  – melodic style: eg close to speech and moving by step and small leaps; wide-ranging and containing bigger leaps.

- As a class, record comments in the *Songwriter's notebook* (*CD-ROM page 8*) about the songs they have experienced in this unit or which are current favourites, and what makes them effective.

Teaching tips

- Help the groups be clear about the brief during activities 2 and 3.

- Groups may use the lyrics they created for the class song as their starting point if they wish.

- Groups working on a verse and chorus structure may find it helpful to start by creating lyrics for a strong memorable chorus, leaving the informative content of their song to the verses.

- Emphasise that this is a process and that songs emerge through trying out ideas and revising them.

- Help the groups to get started by suggesting a pattern of repetition and contrast, eg a protest song group might take the structure of *Children of Africa*; a descriptive song group might use the structure in *Ocean of mystery*.

- Rhyming schemes can be restricting and may result in a stilted, forced effect. Encourage the children to use rhyme only if it is not getting in the way of their creativity.

3 Draft lyrics for the group song

- When each group has collected a word bank, they decide on:
  – a song structure to work within (*eg verse and chorus*); (*each section of the song should be at least four lines long*).

- On copies of the *Lyrics and melody* photocopiable they draft a first set of lyrics containing four lines in which
  – at least one line is repeated.

- The group drafts and redrafts their lyrics, referring frequently to their brief to check that they are fulfilling its requirements, eg

  – that the lyrics of a crowd protest song have a clear structure of repetition for easy participation;

  – that the lyrics of a descriptive song create strong images of the subject.

- They share their ideas with the class, inviting constructive feedback.

- They record their work in progress on copies of the *Lyrics and melody* photocopiable, and store them in the group *Songwriter's notebook*.

2 Explain the brief for a new group song commission

- Explain that groups are going to compose songs to enter into a class song contest in which there will be several awards (*see Lesson 6 activity 3 for examples*). They may choose to write either of these:

  – a protest song to sing to an audience, or to march to;

  – a descriptive song about the environment.

The song must contain at least four lines of lyrics and four lines of melody (*including repetitions*).

- Help the class form itself into groups of four or five according to preferred song style: protest or descriptive song.

- Explain that the songs will be judged on:

  – the lyrics: whether they achieve their intended impact; how clear or informative the message is; the expressiveness of particular words, the images created, the mood inspired;

  – the melody: how well it supports the mood of the lyrics; how well it achieves a purpose such as inspiring participation, or holding the audience's silent attention;

  – the accompaniment: whether it supports the song or detracts in some way.

- The groups may need access to the class *Songwriter's notebook* for ideas, and should begin compiling a group notebook in which to record their work in progress and final song.

- They choose their protest issue or subject for description, and start brainstorming words and phrases associated with them, noticing rhymes which might be useful later.

- They make a bank of words and phrases in their group *Songwriter's notebook* (*CD-ROM page 9*).

Lyrics and melody

Song title _____

Lyrics structure

A

melody

lyrics

Melody structure

A

Songwriter
Exploring lyrics and melody

KEEP DRAFTING

1 Draft melody lines for the group song

- In the same songwriting groups from Lesson 4, the children choose a set of notes to work with, eg

C D E G A	F# G B♭ C'	D E F G A B C' D'

- They try out initial melody ideas for their four lines of lyrics in which:
  - at least one melody line is repeated (*it need not be the same as the repeated lyric line*).
- They sing and play the lyrics and melody, making changes if required.
- Each group plays the first draft of their song to the class and receives evaluation and suggestions for improvement.
- They record their revised drafts on copies of the *Lyrics and melody* photocopiable, storing them in their *Songwriter's notebook*.

2 Consider an accompaniment style for the group song

- All listen to tracks 42, 43, 44, 49 and 51 and focus on the different styles of accompaniment which have been created, eg
  - drone and steady beat (*Children of Africa* track 42);
  - strummed guitar chords (*Nowhere else to go* track 43);
  - rhythmic ostinato on percussion (*Same or different game* track 44);
  - melodic ostinato on tuned percussion (*Ocean of mystery* track 49);
  - atmospheric free sounds, eg wind and pebbles on shore (*Ocean of mystery* track 49);
  - body and vocal percussion (*Sweeping the streets* improvisation track 51).

- The songwriting groups consider what style of accompaniment is appropriate to their song, eg if they are writing a protester's march song, they may need to create something with a strong, marching beat, while a descriptive piece of songwriting might be better suited to atmospheric sounds.
- Encourage the groups to use any of the ideas above, or create something new. Give them time and resources to try out their ideas.
- Invite each group to perform its emerging song accompaniment to the rest of the class for evaluation and suggested improvements. They jot down their ideas in the *Songwriter's notebook*, (CD-ROM page 10).

3 Bring it all together

- The groups now need to combine their draft song with their chosen accompaniment style.
- Give the groups as many opportunities as they need to perform their work to the rest of the class for feedback.

YOURVISION SONG CONTEST

1 Complete the new song arrangements

- The songwriting groups revise what they worked on in the last lesson, and practise their accompaniment. They may need to work out each other's roles, eg
  - will they all sing or will one person sing solo while the others join in with a chorus;
  - who will accompany?
  - will one person direct the group or will everyone listen to each other to ensure they perform well together?

- The groups rehearse their song performance, recording the rehearsals, listening back, noticing what needs improving, and constantly working on improvements.

2 Refine the group songs using audience feedback

- After the rehearsals in activity 1, the groups perform to the class. *(If appropriate, the group teaches their song to the class.)* The class give their reactions, commenting on:
  - the lyrics: what was the impact of words and phrases, the clarity of the message or information contained, the expressiveness of particular words, the images created, the mood inspired?
  - the melody: how well did it support the lyrics in conveying the desired effect? Did it achieve an end such as inspiring participation, or hold the audience's silent attention?
  - the accompaniment: was it an appropriate support to the song or did it detract in any way?
  - the whole song: did it affect the audience in the intended way?

- Using class feedback, the groups refine their songs and make a clean copy, using the template on CD-ROM page 11 if appropriate.

3 Stage the *Yourvision Song Contest*

- Give everyone a final opportunity to rehearse their song, then invite a panel of judges to hear all the songs and award prizes in categories such as:
  - Best protest song lyrics
  - Best descriptive song lyrics
  - Best protest song melody
  - Best descriptive song melody
  - Best accompaniment
  - Best single line of lyrics
  - Best single line of melody
  - Best song overall

  (Make sure there are enough categories and prizes to recognise everyone's achievements. Use the certificates on CD-ROM pic 12.)

- Record the performances onto cassette or onto CD if appropriate software and recording equipment is available *(see Music Express website for links)*, and compile a class *Yourvision Songbook*.

INTRODUCING A CAT AND A MOUSE

1 Read and discuss the poems, *Cats* and *Mice*

- Write the poems *Cats* and *Mice* on the board, read them, and discuss what they are about.

Cats sleep anywhere,
Any table, any chair,
Top of piano, window ledge,
In the middle, on the edge.
Open drawer, empty shoe,
Anybody's lap will do,
Fitted in a cardboard box,
In the cupboard with your frocks.
Anywhere! They don't care!
Cats sleep anywhere.

Their tails are long, their faces small,
They haven't any chins at all,
I think mice are rather nice.
Their ears are pink, their teeth are white,
They run about the house at night,
I think mice are rather nice.
They nibble things they shouldn't touch,
And no-one seems to like them much.
But I think mice are nice!

- Notice the lines of the poems which are repeated.
  (*'Cats sleep anywhere' is repeated at the end. 'I think mice are rather nice' occurs every third line.*)

- Ask what characteristics of cats and mice come out most strongly in the poems.
  (*Cats – eg lazy, sleepy, uncaring, unfussy; mice – eg small, fast, cute, neat.*)

- Invite volunteers to recite each of the poems in ways which express the characteristics you have identified.

Background information

- *Cats* is by Eleanor Farjeon (1881–1965), poet, lyricist and playwright. Her best-known lyrics are *Morning has broken*.
- *Mice* is by Rose Fyleman (1877–1957), a contemporary of Eleanor Farjeon. She is famous for writing the line: 'there are fairies at the bottom of my garden'.
- *Cat and mouse games* was composed by Malcolm Abbs in 1995. It uses the words of Eleanor Farjeon and Rose Fyleman's poems.

2 Discuss the musical setting of *Cat and mouse games*

- All listen to *Cat and mouse games* (track 52). Discuss how the composer has made the two poems into one song.
  (*He has written one tune for Cats which we hear first, and a different one for Mice, heard second; they both fit together as partner songs, at the end.*)

- Ask the children to describe the style of the song.
  (*The tempo is quite fast. A piano plays an um-cha um-cha pattern all the way through. The mood is quite cheerful.*)

- Listen again and ask the children to describe the *Cats* and *Mice* melodies.
  (*The rhythms and phrases of both melodies are quite simple and repetitive. The Cats melody moves along smoothly, sliding across a small range of notes. The Mice melody sounds more jaunty, quick and neat. The rhythm of 'I think mice are rather nice' is made up of longer notes than the rest of either melody ...*)

- Ask what makes this song exciting.
  (*The catchy, jaunty melodies; the way they fit together at the end; the cheerful, bright sound; the um-cha accompaniment ...*)

3 Learn to sing two phrases from *Cats*

- Explain that the *Cats* melody uses two phrases which are repeated and varied throughout. Listen to them on track 53, and copy-sing them in the gaps after each phrase. Notice that each starts just after the first beat:

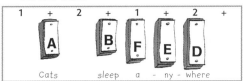

- Invite volunteers to play the two phrases on any tuned instruments available (*tuned percussion, keyboard, piano, recorder*). Give as many children as possible opportunities to play.

- Practise singing the phrases without the CD, aiming for accuracy. Use the tuned instruments to check your pitch.

Teaching tips

- As you sing each phrase, trace the pitch movement with your hand, noticing the downward leap in the first phrase.

ALL ABOUT CATS

1 Revise *Cats*

- Revise the two *Cats* phrases learnt in Lesson 1 activity 3.

- All listen to the complete *Cats* melody on track 54. Count how many times the first phrase occurs. *(Six times.)*

  Discuss how it is sometimes varied.
  (The rhythm of the first two notes is altered to fit different numbers of syllables in subsequent lyrics, eg first time – 'Cats sleep', second time – 'Any table'. The rhythm is drawn out to bring the song to a close.)

- Listen again to track 54 and count how many times the second phrase occurs. *(Four times.)*

  Ask how this phrase is varied.
  (Again, the beginning of the phrase is varied rhythmically to accommodate different numbers of syllables.)

- Write the lyrics on the board, and teach the song using track 55 *(this track repeats each line for the children to listen to then copy).*

Teaching tips

- Remind everyone that the phrases start just after the strong beat so they need to be ready to start together and to take a breath in time.

- Articulate the words clearly, eg the 'c' of 'cats'; the 'ts' and 'sl' of 'cats sleep'; quick words such as 'open drawer'; long syllables at the end of phrases like 'ledge', 'edge', 'box' and 'socks'.

- Sustain vowel sounds for their full length; do not reach the consonants 'dg' (of 'ledge' and 'edge') and 'cks' (of 'box' and 'socks') too soon.

2 Learn untuned percussion accompaniments for *Cats*

- All learn each of the four untuned percussion parts on the **Untuned cats** photocopiable *(triangle, jingle bells, cymbal, guiro)*, by miming playing each instrument in turn with track 56.

- Allocate as many of the four instruments as are available, and practise accompanying the song with the **Untuned cats** accompaniment. *(Those without instruments continue to mime, or join in singing the song quietly.)*

- Pass the instruments round to give everyone opportunities to play at least one of the parts.

3 Rehearse singing *Cats* with the untuned percussion accompaniment

- Divide the class into two groups to rehearse the song *Cats* with track 56: one group sings the song while the other group performs the four untuned percussion parts practised in activity 2.

  As you practise, focus on:

  – singing and playing in time with each other;

  – performing with expression;

  – a good balance between the volume of all the parts.

- Swap parts to give everyone opportunities to sing and play.

Photocopiable

Untuned cats

I	+	2	+	I	+	2	+	I	+	2	+	I	+	2	+

Introduction --
(first time only)

Cats sleep...

CATS AND MICE

1 Learn to sing *Mice*

- Explain that the *Mice* melody also uses two phrases which are repeated and varied throughout.

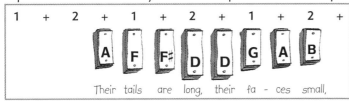

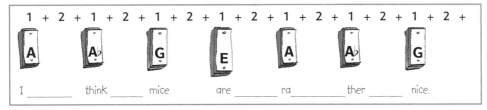

- All listen to track 57 and count how many times each phrase occurs. *(The first phrase occurs six times, and the second occurs three times.)*

  Ask how each phrase is varied.
  (Sometimes the first note of the first phrase is short and other times it is long. Also, sometimes the first note is an E not an A. The second phrase is always the same until the final time when it is shortened to end the song.)

- Write the lyrics on the board and teach the song using track 58 *(this track repeats each line for the children to listen to and then copy).*

  As you sing each line, trace the pitch movement with your hand. Practise pitching the melody as accurately as possible.

Teaching tips

- Notice that the first word comes just before the strong beat; the children need to be ready to breathe.
- Remind the children to articulate the words clearly, particularly 'I think mice are rather nice'.
- The syllables 'I', 'think', 'are', 'ra-', and '–ther' are each sustained. Make sure that the '-nk' of 'think' comes at the end of the sustained long note.

3 Combine parts of the performance

- Rehearse singing the song *Cats* followed by *Mice* with the first part of track 52. Make sure everyone can sing both songs from memory.

- Invite individuals or groups to demonstrate their work in progress from activity 2. Encourage the class to give feedback and suggest improvements.

- Explore combining some of the ideas rehearsed so far *(eg accompany each song with any or all of the untuned or tuned percussion parts).*

2 Work individually and in groups on ideas for the final performance

- Give the children the opportunity to try different accompaniment ideas for the song, in addition to those learnt last lesson.

  Working individually or in groups, give everyone a choice of:

  - practising accompaniments from the *Untuned mice*, *Melodic mice* and *Tuneful cats* photocopiables, tracks 59, 60 and 61 respectively;

  - practising the violin, cello, flute, descant recorder and clarinet parts from the CD-ROM;

  - composing an instrumental prelude to the song, entitled 'Sleepy cats and meddlesome mice';

  - devising movement and dance ideas for part of the performance.

Teaching tips

- Children who have violin, cello, flute, clarinet or recorder lessons could take the parts (printed out from the CD-ROM) to their next instrumental lesson to practise. They may also practise by playing along with tracks 56, and 59–61 on the CD.

- Children who choose to work on a composition should consider the personalities of cats and mice as described in the poem, and how this might be reflected musically.

  They should also consider how their music might lead into the song.

Untuned mice

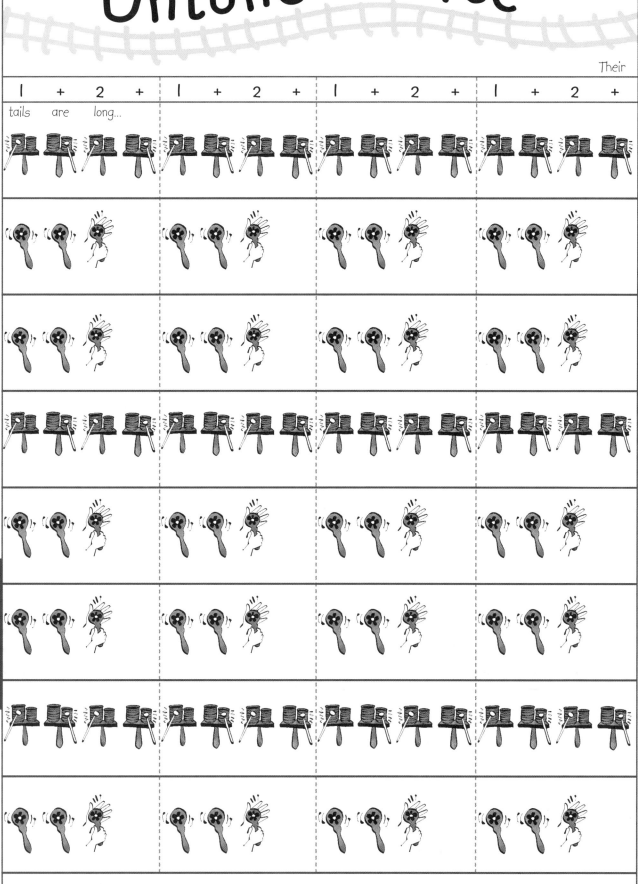

Their

1	+	2	+	1	+	2	+	1	+	2	+	1	+	2	+

tails   are   long...

Melodic mice

1	+	2	+	1	+	2	+	1	+	2	+	1	+	2	+

Introduction --

F	F#	D		G	run beater up xylophone from G			F	F#	D		G	run beater up xylophone from G		
A				A♭				G				E	run beater up xylophone from E		
A				A♭				G				E	run beater up xylophone from E		
F	F#	D		G	run beater up xylophone from G			F	F#	D		G	run beater up xylophone from G		
A				A♭				G				E	run beater up xylophone from E		
A				A♭				G				E	run beater up xylophone from E		
F	F#	D		G	run beater up xylophone from G			F	F#	D		G	run beater up xylophone from G		
A				A♭		G		F#				D	run beater up xylophone from D		

Music Express Year 5 © A & C Black 2003
www.acblack.com/musicexpress

Tuneful cats

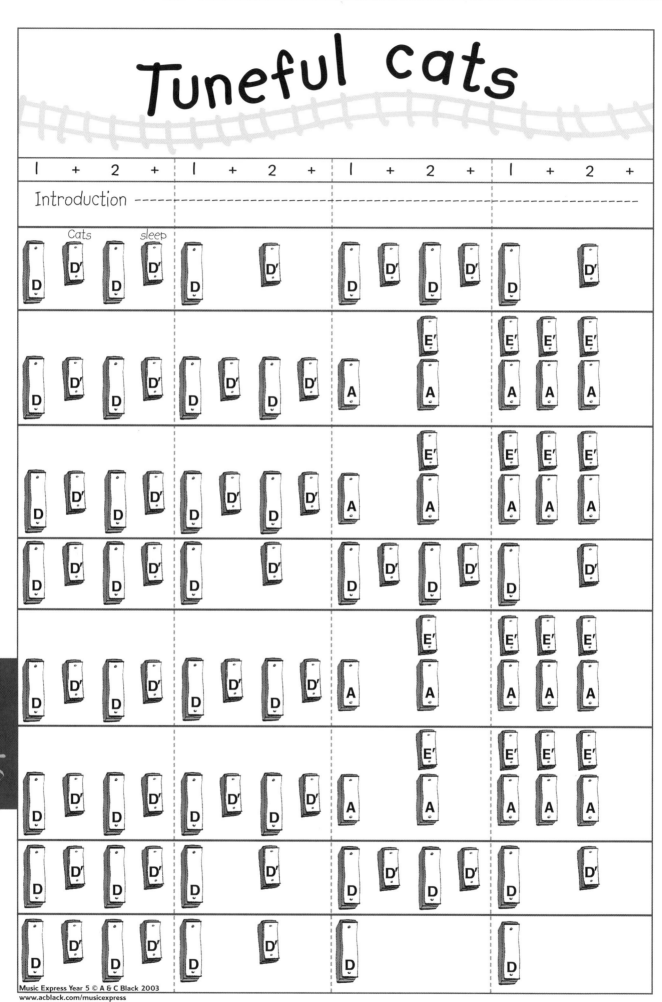

MORE CATS AND MICE

1 Practise singing the song all the way through

- Rehearse the song all the way through, firstly with track 52 and then, when confident, with backing track 62. All sing *Cats* followed by *Mice* in unison, then split into two groups to combine *Cats* and *Mice*.

- When everyone can sing the song all the way through, combining *Cats* and *Mice* confidently, start paying more attention to the following:

  - articulating the words clearly;
  - singing with expression and enjoyment;
  - singing the song in musical phrases;
  - the balance between the two voice parts when singing the partner songs at the end *(it should not sound like a competition in volume between the two groups)*;
  - making sure the two groups synchronise saying the words 'Cats' and 'Mice' together at the end.

Teaching tips
- Make sure there are some confident singers in each group to help lead the others.
- This song is quite long and very repetitive. Encourage everyone to maintain their concentration throughout.
- Appoint a group of children to listen to a rehearsal and give feedback.

2 Record a performance of the complete song and discuss the results

- Record the class singing the song all the way through with backing track 62.

- Listen back to the recording with the children. Ask them to write down:
  - what sounded good;
  - what didn't sound so good;
  - what requires more work and attention;
  - what suggestions they have on how to improve the performance.

- Discuss everyone's ideas, and practise the areas requiring work.

3 Continue work on contributions to the performance

- Decide as a class who will perform what in the final performance. Consider:
  - whether you will perform with or without the backing track;
  - how many singers are needed for each song and who they will be;
  - which accompaniment ideas to include, making sure the singing is always clear;
  - whether there is a composition idea which the class considers effective to start the performance;
  - whether there are any dance ideas which the class considers effective to include in the performance;
  - whether a conductor will be needed for the performance.

- If there is a composition or dance group, give them the opportunity to rehearse separately, and then perform their ideas to the class. Again, the class suggests any improvements needed.

Everyone else should practise different combinations of singing with percussion and/or instrumental accompaniments.

PREPARE TO PERFORM

1 **Discuss non-musical factors that contribute to a good performance, and make a performance plan**

- As a class think about when and where you will be performing the song. Discuss:

  - The performance space
    Is it big or small? Is the audience near to or far away from the performers? Is there a stage?

  - Dress code
    What should you wear – school uniform, all wearing the same but not school uniform, eg coloured shirts, costumes?

- Decide a plan for the performance and write it down with as much detail as possible to remember for next week. Here is a sample plan:

Sleepy cats and meddlesome mice	List of performers + details of instruments they are playing Details of where they will perform
Cats	All singers Accompanied by all four Untuned cats parts and the Tuneful cats part – list names and who is playing which instrument
Mice	All singers Accompanied by cello (Lisa) and flute (Toby) and Untuned mice parts - list names and who is playing which instrument
Cats and Mice partner song	Group A sing Cats - list names Group B sing Mice - list names Dancers perform - weaving in and out of the audience Accompanied by cello, flute, Untuned cats and mice as above

- Decide where everyone will be positioned for the performance and who will sit or stand. Check that:

  - everyone will be able to see the conductor (if you are using one);

  - instrumentalists will be able to sit or stand comfortably in order to play without strain;

  - instrumentalists playing from copies of the music can see them comfortably.

  (You might like to sketch a map of the performance area.)

Teaching tips

- The *Performance plan* should contain any information that you want, written in a form that is useful to you, eg who is performing what and when.

- Choose your own notation for the plan: names, words, symbols, pictures, music notation.

- You might need to make alterations to the *Performance plan* as you rehearse.

2 **Put all the parts of the performance together**

- Decide whether children will join in the singing when they are not performing their accompaniment. Make sure everyone is clear about what they are doing and when.

- Rehearse the song all the way through several times until everyone is confident. Check that:

  - everyone comes in at the right time;

  - all parts are performed in time with each other;

  - the balance between all the parts is good, and the singers can be heard clearly;

  - everyone is silent before they start and after they finish.

3 **Make improvements to the performance**

- Continue refining the performance so that all children are giving their best.

CAT AND MOUSE GAMES

1 Hold a dress rehearsal or final run-through

- Set up the performance area – position any chairs, instruments and music stands where needed, and make sure any music parts required are in an appropriate place.
  (Make sure the performance area looks tidy.)

- Have a walk-through rehearsal. Practise:

  – walking into the performance area;
  (Practise walking on, in order, quietly and efficiently and getting into position sensibly.)

  – acknowledging the applause;
  (Will the conductor bow? How will you acknowledge applause before you perform? Will everyone bow, if so practise bowing at the same time.)

  – starting the song;
  (Practise waiting for silence from the audience and then starting the song.)

  – sitting and holding instruments silently when not playing;
  (Make sure everyone knows when to pick up their instrument so that they are ready to play and can do so as quietly as possible. Practise sitting without fidgeting.)

  – holding the stillness at the end of the performance;
  (Practise the last few notes of the song, and staying still and silent until the applause starts.)

  – acknowledging the applause;
  (Practise all standing up together if seated, and bowing if the children decide they would like to.)

  – walking off the performance area.
  (Practise walking off, in order, quietly and efficiently after the applause has finished.)

Teaching tips

- Remind the children that they only get one chance at a performance and so concentration is all-important.

- Point out that the children are on show the entire time and should be on their best behaviour.

- When you rehearse, notice whether the performance area is particularly echoey. If so, encourage the singers to articulate the words more crisply than usual.

- If any children are bringing instruments in from home to play, ask if their teacher could check they are in tune before the performance.

2 Refine the performance

- Rehearse a performance of the song. Walk into the performance area as rehearsed, but this time rehearse the song as well. Encourage the children to remember to:

  – concentrate and appear focussed on the performance;

  – look as though enjoying the performance;

  – perform with expression;

  – articulate the words clearly;

  – watch the conductor for cues (if you are using one).

- After the rehearsal, give positive feedback and encouragement.

3 Perform the song to an audience

- Perform the song as rehearsed.

- Afterwards, discuss what went well. Ask the children what they considered to be the three best things about the performance.

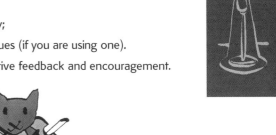

STYLE SKETCHES

1 Listen to three styles of music

- Explain that in this unit the class is going to work with starting points, processes and structures which composers might use to create their music. Finally they will develop a piece of machine music, using what they have learnt about these procedures.

- Throughout the unit, the class will refer to an imaginary composer's sketchbook of starting points for composition. Show the class the *Sketchbook* photocopiable and notice together what the different sketches represent:
    - a sequence of guitar chords;
    - a rhythm;
    - graphic representations of pitch;
    - a number pattern.

- Invite volunteers to demonstrate with their voices, body percussion or instruments how each of the sketches might sound.

- Notice that a sketched starting point gives a very incomplete idea of the sound it represents, eg the rhythm pattern does not show tempo, instrument or manner of performance. Explain that composers need to think about what they will do with an initial idea, and in particular:
    - what mood and effect they want to create.

- Look at the guitar chords on the photocopiable and then listen to tracks 1–3 to hear three extracts of music, all based on the same chords. Discuss how the three extracts differ in mood, eg
    - first: rock style – played very fast, quite loudly on electric guitar;
    - second: heavy metal style – played at a steady tempo, very loudly on electric guitar with distortion effect and pitch bend;
    - third: country style – played at a relaxed tempo, fairly quietly on a metal-stringed acoustic guitar.

- Invite the children to describe the mood of the styles in terms such as: energetic, fast, relaxed, harsh, exciting, soothing, etc.

3 Choose instruments for three different styles of music

- Listen to track 1 and revise the three riffs the children chose to accompany it in activity 2.

- From as wide a selection of instruments as possible, invite the class to choose one for each of the chosen riffs, carefully considering the timbre of each instrument and its suitability. Invite three children to practise playing one riff each along with the track.

- Together, evaluate the effectiveness of the instrumental timbres and change as necessary.

- Having selected suitable instruments, consider how loudly or quietly they should be played, trying out different volumes with the music. Notice whether the way the instrument is played has an effect on the sound, for instance a drum can be played with gentle strokes or hard, sharp taps.

- Add this information to the riffs in the sketchbook: the chosen instrument, the appropriate volume, and manner of playing.

- Repeat with tracks 2 and 3.

- Discuss what the children have learnt about different styles of music, noting how tempo, timbre, volume and performance are all important in creating moods and effects.

Background information

- Probably the most famous Western European composer to keep a sketchbook was Beethoven (1770-1827). He kept a desk sketchbook by his piano for jotting down ideas as he was working and a pocket sketchbook which he carried around with him at all times.

- Sketches can take the form of pictures, written memos, sound words, staff notation, graphic notation – whatever serves to remind the composer of an idea.

- A 'sketchbook' might also be a pocket audio recorder for collecting sounds.

2 Perform rhythms in three different styles

- Listen to track 1 again and invite the children to join in, making up repeated rhythms with body percussion or tapping fingers on desktops.

    Encourage the children to close their eyes as they play, and to feel their way into the style of the music through the rhythms they tap or sing.

- Ask the class how they found themselves playing, eg did the music inspire them to play:
    - active, energetic, fast rhythms?
    - slow, heavy rhythms?
    - calm, relaxed, quiet rhythms?

- Invite individuals to demonstrate rhythms they have used to accompany the track. As a class decide on three rhythms to use as riffs and find a way to notate them in a class sketchbook. (*Sound words are a useful device for notating rhythms, eg boom chicka chick, or bo-bop shawady-wady.*)

- Repeat for tracks 2 and 3.

Teaching tips

- Use a scrapbook or flipchart for the class sketchbook.

- Encourage the children to explore different ways of sketching their ideas, using symbols, words, pictures, musical notation.

- The children will have opportunities to use the sketchbook throughout the rest of this unit.

- Riff has a similar meaning to ostinato – a repeated pattern.

Sketchbook

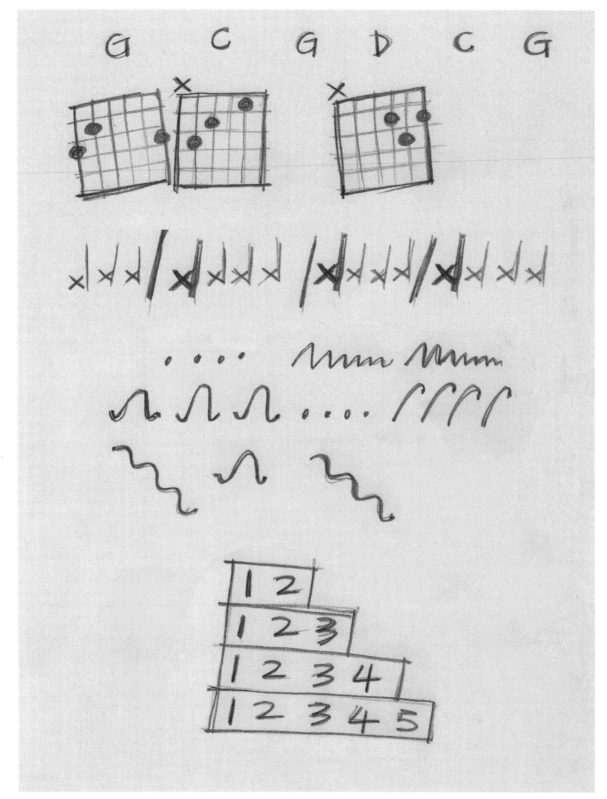

TRAIN SKETCHES

1 Listen to *Rhapsody in blue*

- Listen to the opening extract of *Rhapsody in blue*. Explain that the composer's starting points included knowing that he had to write for:
  - a concert to promote jazz;
  - solo piano and jazz orchestra;
  In addition he was inspired by:
  - a painting;
  - the rhythm of a steam train.

- Listen again noticing these two ideas:
  - *the main melody played first on clarinet then on other instruments, sometimes one, sometimes several*
  - *the 'train' rhythm played by the brass instruments.*

3 Improvise melodies to add to the train composition

- Listen to track 5, noticing that there are eight clicks underlying each improvised section – these mark the tempo and the length of the improvisation.

- All clap or tap the train rhythm together and invite someone to tap a woodblock quietly eight times between each repeat of the rhythm:

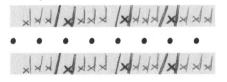

- When this is secure, set out tuned percussion notes:

  G A B♭ B C' D' E'

  Invite an individual to improvise melodically and rhythmically during the gaps between the train rhythm, played four times.

- Give several children practice at improvising.

- When the children are comfortable with improvising in this way, discuss how the mood of the music might be altered, eg
  - by playing at a faster/slower tempo; louder/quieter;
  - by playing faster or slower improvisations;
  - by playing in a calm, relaxed manner/highly energetic manner...

- Decide on a mood for a performance of the train rhythm on instruments as in activity 2, with someone improvising in the gaps.

Background information

George Gershwin composed *Rhapsody in blue* in 1924, working to a very tight deadline. He improvised much of the solo piano part during the first performance, later notating it, following the instant success of the piece.

2 Choose instruments to play Gershwin's train rhythm

- Show the children the sketch of Gershwin's train rhythm on the *Sketchbook* photocopiable (*below the guitar chord sequence*).

- Notice that this sketch simply shows the train rhythm. Ask the children to suggest what else it might show, eg
  - instruments;
  - tempo and volume (*how fast/slow it is, how loud/quiet*);
  - manner of playing (*whether smooth, gentle, harsh*).

- Listen to track 5 on which the train rhythm is played four times. The rhythm is followed each time by melodic improvisations similar in style to Gershwin's own:

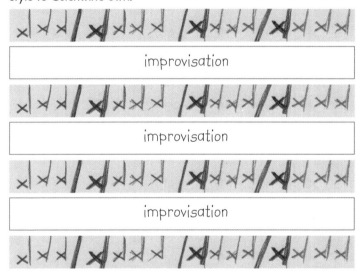

- Discuss how you would like to orchestrate (*choose instruments for*) each repetition of the train rhythm, deciding when the instruments will play singly, in small groups, or all together. Choose freely from a wide selection of instruments, aiming to select appropriate, effective timbres.

- Notate the order in which the instruments play in the class sketchbook, displaying it where it can be seen by the players. Play track 5 and accompany it with the chosen instruments.

- As a class, evaluate the musical effect, making changes to instruments, volume and manner of playing until satisfied, then noting them in the sketchbook.

Teaching tips
- The train music is in rondo form, a commonly used musical structure which has sections A B A C A D A.
- Take care to keep the tempo steady, and keep marking the beat quietly with a woodblock during the improvisations.

DAWN SKETCHES

1 Listen to *Le réveil des oiseaux*

- Listen to *Le réveil des oiseaux*, explaining that the composer's inspiration was birdsong and that the piece progresses in time from the birds' awakening at dawn through to midday (*this extract is from the busy mid-morning section of the birds' chorus*).

  Listen again, noticing:

  - the careful choice of instruments to represent the birdsongs;

  - differences in volume which give a sense of space, some birds being further away than others;

  - the way the performers play their instruments in a very bird-like manner;

  - the way the sounds are heard singly or in overlapping combinations.

- All look at the sketches of birdsong on the *Sketchbook* photocopiable (*below the train rhythm*). Invite volunteers to suggest vocal sounds or whistles to interpret the sketches.

- Using real or imaginary birdsongs or those represented in *Le réveil des oiseaux*, devise birdsong graphics in the class sketchbook, showing as carefully as you can the pitches of each call. Invite individuals to vocalise or whistle each call, checking that the graphics are good representations of the sound.

Background information

- The French composer Messiaen (1908-1992) collected recordings of birdsongs which he then represented in several of his compositions.

- Messiaen wrote *Le réveil des oiseaux* (*The Awakening of the birds*) in 1953. The piece contains references to the songs of 38 French birds.

2 Organise birdsong ideas from the class sketchbook into timed structures

- Invite three individuals to select one birdsong each from the graphic notations in the class sketchbook.

- Explain that the same three individuals are going to demonstrate ways of organising their birdsongs to create a piece of music that lasts twenty seconds. Show the class the *Birdsong structures* photocopiable, and appoint a timekeeper to count the seconds very quietly for the performers:

  Structure 1: Sequence

  - 0–5 seconds: the first child performs;

  - 5–10 seconds: the second child performs, and so on

  Structure 2: Layering – overlapping

  - the performers begin at five second intervals and perform for ten seconds each.

  Structure 3: Layering – adding and subtracting

  - one performer plays throughout, while the other two enter and exit after shorter periods of time.

- Discuss as a class the effectiveness of each structure in giving an impression of birdsong in the natural environment. Invite alternative suggestions and try them out.

3 Create group compositions depicting the dawn chorus and record performances

- Divide into groups, giving each a copy of the birdsong page from the class sketchbook. Explain that the groups will create their own piece of birdsong music to depict dawn. The piece must last one minute, and the groups will each appoint their own timekeeper.

  The groups may use vocal sounds or instruments (*make a wide selection available, including classroom instruments, environmental soundmakers such as pen cases, which may be blown, or instruments which children are learning to play*).

- The groups select the birdsongs they wish to use, and start working on the structure of their piece, eg

  - extending one of the structures explored in activity 2;

  - joining two or more of the structures into a sequence;

  - creating a new structure of their own.

- Give the groups time and space in which to rehearse their timed compositions, circulating among them to offer support and help where required. Encourage the groups to create a score of their work which, as on the photocopiable, shows a timeline and the durations of each birdsong.

- The groups perform their work in progress to the class, inviting their evaluation and suggestions for improvement, eg

  - choice of instruments;

  - interpretations of the graphics;

  - effective variations in volume;

  - clarity of structure.

- Record final performances of each group's composition.

Birdsong structures

Structure 1: Sequence

	0 sec	5 sec	10 sec	15 sec	20 sec

Bird 1

Bird 2

Bird 3

Structure 1: Layering – overlapping

	0 sec	5 sec	10 sec	15 sec	20 sec

Bird 1

Bird 2

Bird 3

Structure 2: Layering – adding and subtracting

	0 sec	5 sec	10 sec	15 sec	20 sec

Bird 1

Bird 2

Bird 3

Music Express Year 5 © A & C Black 2003
www.acblack.com/musicexpress

NUMBER SKETCHES

1 Listen to *Zub-a-doo*

- Listen to *Zub-a-doo*, explaining that the composer's starting point is metre – the grouping of beats. The beats in the composition are grouped in threes, fours and fives:

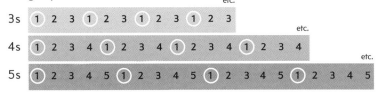

- Listen to *Zub-a-doo* again and tap the beat with fingers on knees, ignoring everything else that is happening in the music. What do the children notice? (*The beat is always the same; it is constant; the first beat is always played louder.*)

- As you or one of the children tap a constant beat on a woodblock, volunteers take turns to tap each metre in turn using body percussion:

  3s knees clap clap knees clap clap...
  4s knees clap clap clap knees clap clap clap...
  5s knees clap clap clap clap knees clap clap clap clap...

  Notice the effect of grouping the beats into threes, fours and fives like this. Each metre has a very different feel.

- Listen to track 8, in which the beats are counted out loud, and all follow the score on the *Zub-a-doo* photocopiable. Listen again, joining in counting the beats and accentuating number one in each group.

- Perform the body percussion patterns in threes, fours and fives as you listen to track 8 again. Repeat the activity until the metres feel familiar.

  (*Invite some confident individuals to join in using untuned percussion.*)

3 Add vocal rhythm patterns to the metric music

- In the groups from activity 2, the children rehearse the metric music they have created on the chosen instruments, using the paper strips score to remind them of the order.

- All listen to track 7, noticing what else the composer adds to the music. (*There are vocal riffs, and melodic phrases.*) Listen again and join in with the vocal riffs.

- Each group works on vocal riffs to add to their composition, trying out different suggestions, and picking one to feature along with each metre.

- The groups perform to the class, inviting feedback on the effectiveness of their metric music – does it have a good overall structure, does the sequence of metres work well, are the vocal riffs rhythmically interesting and fun?

  (*Remind the class that this composition relies on a very steady pulse, contrasts being achieved through the shifts from one metre to another and the interesting vocal riffs.*)

- Ask each group to consider the mood of their piece, and to make alterations as necessary to the instrumentation, manner of performance, tempo and volume in order to enhance the effect they want to achieve.

- Discuss the procedure the children have followed in order to create their music. Paste some examples of the paper strip scores into the class sketchbook for later reference.

Background information

- In *Zub-a-doo*, by Stephen Chadwick, the beat is the key feature of the music.

- Metre is a term used to describe the grouping of beats into twos, threes, fours, etc.

- In *Zub-a-doo* the metre changes in a pre-determined pattern, which gives the composition its structure.

2 Begin composing music using two different metres

- In groups, the children choose two metres to feature in a piece of metric music, eg 4 and 3, or 5 and 2.

- The groups practise playing the metres on body percussion, eg for twos:

  knees clap knees clap knees clap...

  (*Appoint one person in each group to keep the beat on a woodblock, ensuring that it neither speeds up nor slows down.*)

- Each group writes the numbers of their metres on strips of paper, making several copies of each.

- Next they organise the strips of paper into an agreed sequence and try out its effect using body percussion. The groups keep re-ordering the paper strips until they arrive at a sequence they like, fixing it by attaching the paper strips to a backing sheet.

- Listen to track 7 again, noticing the instruments the composer uses to play the constant beat and the strong first beats.

  Distribute a range of percussion instruments to each group (*or take turns to share them*), and invite the children to play their sequence on instruments instead of body percussion, choosing effective sounds to emphasise the strong beats and the constant beat.

Teaching tip

Notice the five silent beats near the end of *Zub-a-doo*. Encourage the children to try out a similar silent break in their metric music – taking care where they place the break to make the best use of the contrast.

Zub-a-doo

1 2 3 4 5	1 2 3	1 2 3
1 2 3 4 5	1 2 3	1 2 3
1 2 3 4 5	1 2 3	1 2 3
1 2 3 4 5	1 2 3	1 2 3

1 2 3 4	1 2 3 4
1 2 3 4	1 2 3 4
1 2 3 4	1 2 3 4
1 2 3 4	1 2 3 4

1 2 3 4 5	1 2 3	1 2 3
1 2 3 4 5	1 2 3	1 2 3
1 2 3 4 5	1 2 3	1 2 3
1 2 3 4 5	1 2 3	1 2 3

1 2 3 4	1 2 3 4
1 2 3 4	1 2 3 4
1 2 3 4	1 2 3 4
1 2 3 4	1 2 3 4

1 2 3 4 5	1 2 3	1 2 3
1 2 3 4 5	1 2 3	1 2 3
1 2 3 4 5	1 2 3	1 2 3

| 1 2 3 4 5 | 1 2 3 4 5 | 1 2 3 | 1 2 3 |

MACHINE SKETCH

1 Explore starting points and procedures for composing a piece of machine music

p60

- Explain that the children are going to create a piece of machine music in three stages: 1 initial ideas, 2 development, 3 structure.

  Referring to the four previous lessons, discuss what the children have discovered about:

  - initial ideas (that they can be inspired by anything);

  - processes for developing ideas: choosing instruments, improvising, creating rhythms, pitch, metre; remembering that the mood of the music is further enhanced by choice of tempo, dynamics, and manner of playing;

  - structures, eg repetition and contrast (eg ABA), rondo (ABACADA), sequences, layers, cycles.

- Divide the class into groups and explain that their brief is to compose a piece of music:
  - using machinery as the starting point;
  - lasting two minutes;
  - using any available sound sources;
  - for performance at an assembly.

- Give the groups large sheets of paper on which to sketch out their ideas, and give each a copy of the *Machine sketches* photocopiable. As a class, discuss the ideas on the photocopiable:

  - instruments: which of these might be useful? Can real machinery sound sources be used? (*eg metronome, clock, mechanical parts, metal cogs and ratchets*);

  - metre: might two or more metres be used in sequence or in combinations? Would it be appropriate for there to be no pulse? Can word rhythms be used as riffs? What other word rhythms or word sounds are suggested by the machinery?

  - pitch: how might melodic patterns be used, eg as ostinatos or melodies;

  - mood and effect: which words best describe what the groups want to achieve and how will they create this?

- Give the groups a set time in which to sketch out their initial ideas and agree the processes for developing them, eg word rhythms to be developed into riffs, alternated with free improvisations.

3 Groups demonstrate and record work in progress to remember for the next lesson

- Encourage each group to discuss and sketch out a possible structure for their machine music, reminding them of some of the structures they might use:

  - repetition and contrast, eg the train rhythms rondo (ABACADA) in Lesson 2;

  - the timed sequences and layers in Lesson 3;

  - the number patterns in Lesson 4.

- Using the instruments and sound sources they have chosen, the groups begin to try out their ideas within the selected structure.

- As they work, they make notes about instrumentation, style, tempo, volume, manner of play on the sketch pages. If time allows they make a score which shows the complete structure, and incorporates decisions from earlier sketches.

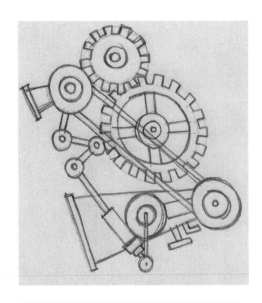

Teaching tips
- Make the class sketchbook available for reference.
- Too much choice may be confusing for some groups. If so, limit their choice and tighten the brief, eg prescribe three word rhythms, three pitches, three instruments, two metres and two contrasting sections which share a constant sound.

2 Groups begin to develop their machine compositions

- The groups refer to the sketches they have made and the process they have chosen for development. They try out their ideas on the selected instruments or sound sources.

- Invite each group to demonstrate their work in progress to the class, encouraging a representative from each to explain the procedures which have been adopted.

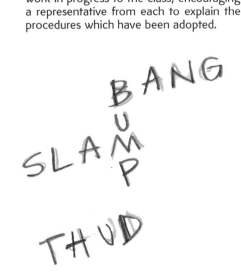

Who knows?
Exploring musical processes

Photocopiable

Machine sketches

www.acblack.com/musicexpress

60

IT'S INSPIRED!

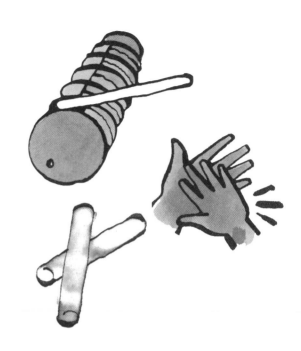

1 Groups continue developing their machine compositions

- Each group assimilates the feedback from the last lesson into their machine composition and, if they haven't already done so, they now create a score to show the structure of their composition, incorporating all important directions and information such as instrumentation, mood, tempo, and volume.

- Each group then rehearses their work, checking that they are meeting the time requirement of the brief, and working on details of performance such as playing together as a group, following the directions of a conductor if they are using one, playing techniques, and overall mood.

- Invite a representative from each group to explain to the class the initial ideas and the process the group has used to create their machine composition. Another child from the group should show the class the sketches the children made while developing their ideas, and a third child explains the structure of the piece referring to the group's score. They perform their work and invite feedback.

Teaching tips

- If possible, conduct the final rehearsal in the space where the assembly will be held, so that the children are confident about their positions, and are aware of any effect the larger space will have on the sound they produce (*eg they may need to play more quietly if the acoustic is bright, or more loudly if it is dull.*)

2 The class decide on a final performance order for the machine compositions

- In preparation for the performance of the compositions at assembly, decide on an order for the groups to play in, and rehearse each group in turn, ensuring that:
    - all instruments are ready to hand and properly set up;
    - that the groups can quickly move into position;
    - that the scores are clearly visible if they are required for the performance;
    - that one child from each group can confidently turn to the audience and announce the piece.

- If possible, record the final rehearsal. Listen back to the recording and, as a class, help each group to make final adjustments to their piece.

3 Groups perform their machine compositions))

- Present an assembly on musical inspirations:
    - introduce the assembly with *Lé reveil des oiseaux*, explaining what inspired its composition;
    - play *Rhapsody in blue* and talk about Gershwin's starting ideas;
    - play *Zub-a-doo* and display the score;
    - perform the groups' machine compositions with introductions and brief explanations by group members;
    - invite the audience to listen out for their own personal musical inspiration during the day.

Index

Index of song titles and first lines

Videoclips

Track Contents

Track	Contents
1	African dance movement 1 (pages 11–12)
2	African dance movement 2 (11–12)
3	African dance movement 3 (16)
4	Changing the dance movement with the cue (11)
5	The round game (16)
6	Clusters using instruments (26)
7	Clusters using voices (26)
8	Moon landing (30–33)

NB There are also 15 videoclips for teachers
(see introduction notes p6)

Audio CD track list

Acknowledgements

The authors and publishers would like to thank all the teachers and consultants who assisted in the preparation of this series: Meriel Ascott, Francesca Bedford, Chris Bryant, Yolanda Cattle, Stephen Chadwick, Veronica Clark, Kate Davies, Tania Demidova, Barry Gibson, Veronica Hanke, Jocelyn Lucas, Helen MacGregor, Carla Moss, Danny Monte, Lio Moscardini, Sue Nicholls, Vanessa Olney, Mrs S. Pennington, Marie Penny, Pauline Quinton, Ana Sanderson, Jane Sebba, Heather Scott, Michelle Simpson, Elhadji Sonko, Debbie Townsend and Joy Woodall.

The authors and publishers would like to thank Kevin Graal, Xanthe Jarjou, Debbie Sanders, Elhadji Sonko, Cleveland Watkiss, Michael Haslam, Stephen Chadwick and Vivien Ellis for performing for the recording of this CD. Thanks are also due to all those who performed for previous recordings for A&C Black publications which have been reused in Music Express Year 5.

Special thanks are due to Danny Monte and the Year 6 children of Brunswick Park Primary School for demonstrating and performing for the filming of the CD-ROM videoclips.

The following have kindly granted permission for the inclusion of their copyright materials and recordings in the book and on the CD:

Malcolm Abbs for the music of **Cat and Mouse games** © 1995 Malcolm Abbs.

Sony BMG Music for **Mare tranquilitatis** performed by Vangelis. Courtesy of Sony BMG Music Entertainment (UK) Ltd. Licensed by Sony BMG Commercial Markets UK.

Stephen Chadwick for the music of **Spacescape, Outer space backing track** and **Zub-a-doo** © 2003 Stephen Chadwick/A&C Black Publishers Limited.

Stephen Chadwick for the words of **Sweeping chant** with vocal improvisations and body percussion by Cleveland Watkiss.

Niki Davies for **Ocean of Mystery** © Niki Davies Productions Ltd.

EMI Records Group UK and Ireland for George Gershwin's **Rhapsody in Blue** performed by Daniel Blumenthal and the English Chamber Orchestra and for Cathy Berberian's **Stripsody** from Songs Cathy Sang performed by Linda Hirst and the London Sinfonietta. Licensed courtesy of EMI Records Limited.

David Higham Associates on behalf of Eleanor Farjeon for the poem **Cats** from *The Children's Bells*. Used by kind permission.

Jan Holdstock for **Calypso** © 1980 Jan Holdstock.

Xanthe Jarjou for the research/arrangement of the music **Degu degu degu.**

Nick Keir for the song **Nowhere else to go.**

Random House Inc for the rights in the USA for **Mice** from *Fifty One New Nursery Rhymes* by Rose Fyleman, © 1931,1932, Doubleday, a division of Random House Inc. used by permission of Random House Children's books, a division of Random House Inc.

Ana Sanderson for **The Human Drum Kit** © 1995 Ana Sanderson.

The Society of Authors as the Literary Representative of the estate of Rose Fyleman for the poem **Mice**. Permission granted for the world excluding USA.

Universal Music for **Le réveil des oiseaux** (The awakening of the birds) – Olivier Messiaen. Performed by the Cleveland Orchestra and conducted by Pierre Boulez. Courtesy of Deutsche Grammophon. Part of the Universal Music Group.

Universal Music for György Ligeti **Atmosphères** and Wolfgang Rihm **Départ** performed by the Weiner Philharmonic Orchestra conducted by Claudio Abbado. Courtesy of Deutsche Grammophon. Part of the Universal Music Group.

The following copyright holder has kindly given permission for the inclusion of their copyright material on the CD-ROM:

Moon walking courtesy of NASA.

All other recordings are © 2003 A&C Black.